ADAIR DIARY

THE EARLY YEARS

THE CITY OF ADAIR VILLAGE

A MOSTLY TRUE
COLLABORATIVE
MEMOIR

CHARLINE KING
WANDA TOBIASSEN
JUDI VEDAMUTHU
WITH DELORES POLLARD

ACKNOWLEDGEMENTS: Special thanks to Mike McInally for permission to use headlines, photos and news articles pertaining to the history of this area from both the *Gazette Times* of Corvallis and the *Democrat Herald* of Albany, Marie Kolchek: the *Seattle Times* for the obituary for Eddie Hoops, the City of Adair Village for records and meeting space, the Corvallis-Benton County Public Library, the Albany City Library, the Albany Regional Museum, the Benton Historical Society, the Benton County Records Department archives in the County Court Journals of Benton County Board of Commissioner Minutes, Kevin Perkins at the Benton County Board of Commissioners Office, Julie Yamaka, Managing Editor of Oregon Blue Book at Oregon State Archives. Judy Juntunen on the Calipolia/Kalapuya or Calapoolia Native Americans talk for Adair Living History. Thanks to John H. Baker for his suggestion to research all the U.S. SAGE buildings. (www.radomes.org/museum/) The Oregon Department of Transportation GIS Unit for maps, Steven Rowe for Capehart military housing, www.achp.gov/army-capehartwherry, Mark Phillips, Assistant Dean, at Digital Libraries, UNT (University of Northern Texas) Libraries for the Cyber Cemetery of digitized government archives: digital.library.unt.edu. Denny and Peggy Haney, Mary Hardenbrook, Chuck and Fran Harris, Dick Green, and Dave Campbell for history of Adair Rural Fire Protection, Gary Richards for geocaching information and *I Remember Camp Adair* Facebook page. Dan and Polly Callahan and Pastor Miller for answering our call-out, Mark Farley for design advice and cheers, Danita Pollard, thanks for the black lines and story enthusiasm, Lorraine Ruff, now deceased, for suggestion to use the memoir format. Lucinda Tuttle for early editing and lawyer Richard Ligon for consultation. Jean and Charles Nelson for professional editing and Terry Carr-Wilson for spit-polish edits and a loving glimpse into the nature of Sharkey. Last, many thanks to Alan Rowe for scrupulous research, steady patience and support.

Author: Charline King

Copyright 2016

ISBN: 1530772028

ISBN13: 978-1530772025

Library of Congress Control Number (LCCN) 2016905866

CreateSpace Independent Publishing Platform, North Charleston, SC

Dedicated to all people who are determined to meet the everyday challenge of making the world a better place.

To Gary -
a great history
teacher & enthusiast -
thanks!
J. Delores

Table of Contents

Forward

Judi Vedamuthu 2013

Way back when, before the advent of white men, the mid-Willamette was inhabited by a number of tribes or bands of the Calipolia/Kalapuya or Calapoolia Native Americans. The various bands gave their names to several of the tributary rivers of the Willamette including Tualatin, Santiam and Luckiamute. The combined population of the Kalapuya was about 28,000 prior to the settlement of white pioneers. After some years the population of the Kalapuya had been reduced to less than 2,000 due both to loss of land and harvestable fields to the settlers and to the spread of "white-man's diseases" among the native population. (Juntunen, Judy Rycraft, et al, The World of the Kalapuya: A Native People of Western Oregon. Philomath, OR: Benton County Historical Society and Museum, 2005.)

The early white settlers entered the Willamette Valley during the 1840s and established their farms, many on Donation Claims from the Federal Bureau of Land management (BLM). These farms were passed down in the families and by the 1940s were owned and operated by the great-grandsons and great-great-grandsons of the original settlers.

The area now known as Adair was sown to wheat. The town of Wells was developed along the railroad tract in the flat area east of Coffin Butte. Reportedly, Wells had the first organized school district in Benton County. West of the area along the stage coach line along Soap Creek was the village of Tampico, which had the reputation of being the gambling/gaming center for Benton County. Tampico eventually disappeared after U. S. Highway 99W was built and the stagecoach phased out.

As World War II developed in Europe, the U.S. Army suspected that the United States might be drawn into it and began to look for appropriate areas in which to set up training camps. Officials noted that the terrain and climate in the Willamette Valley were very similar to Germany and France, so they investigated a couple of sites in western Oregon. With the help of some local politicians and businessmen, the army eventually selected the site now known as Adair. (Baker, John H., *Camp Adair: The Story of a World War II Cantonment*. Newport, OR, LAZERQUICK, 2003.) They made preliminary plans for the camp and by 1942 began the construction of

Camp Adair Military Reservation. Camp Adair covered 56,800 acres of farmland, hills and poison oak in the area eight miles north of Corvallis, eight miles south of Monmouth and six miles west of Albany.

Many farmers and their families were removed from their land, to their great consternation and sorrow. At least two towns, Wells and Locust Grove, were emptied and flattened. They were never rebuilt. After the war, all the farmers were offered the chance to repurchase their land; some did, but others had moved on or had died, so new families moved in.

Camp Adair was named for Captain Rodney Adair, son of a prominent family of Astoria, Oregon and a West Point graduate. He served in the Mexican-American war and was killed in 1916 during a heated battle near Carrizal. The area has been known as Camp Adair Military Reservation, Adair Village Student Housing, Adair Air Force station and now The City of Adair Village.

Our specific part of the story begins in the early 1970's with the U. S. Government deeding the Air Force station proper, to private groups, various educational entities, and to Benton County. The Air Force officers' living units, just north of the Air Force station itself, were sold to a developer, A. G. Proctor from Aurora,

Colorado. Proctor refurbished and made habitable all the units and then sold them to interested individuals. The first people to move in were Bill and Charline Carr, coming from the Portland area. They moved to Adair Meadows so that Bill could be closer to his work in Albany on the proviso that if, after one year, Charline still wanted to return to Portland, they would. By the end of that year, they elected to remain in Adair Meadows and never looked back.

Delores Pollard

Buried under old Camp Adair are huge blocks of cement.

Introduction

In 1946 after the war ended and the Army abandoned Camp Adair, the Oregon State Game Commission (renamed the Department of Fish and Wildlife in 1948) acquired nearly 2,000 acres of surplus government land. This included a fire station and several other government buildings that were not yet demolished. The swampy lands of the north cantonment became E.E. Wilson Wildlife Management Area. The cantonment area was razed between 1946 and 1950. What is left of the old road system can still be seen at the E.E. Wilson Wildlife Management Area.

The south end of the cantonment had been the hospital and it was deeded to Oregon State University, as well as some property west of Highway 99W, which was added to the McDonald Forest. The hospital wards were converted into apartments to house 30 faculty and 320 married students during the post-war veteran student boom. This became the first Adair Village. It was closed in 1951. The hospital buildings, consisting of 6 four-room apartments, were sold. Many of them were cut in half and moved to various locations all over the state.

The property reverted to State Fish and Wildlife.

In 1957, as the Cold War heated up, the Oregon Fish and Wildlife deeded back nearly 352 acres to the government for construction of a Semi Automatic Ground Environment (SAGE) Direction Center.

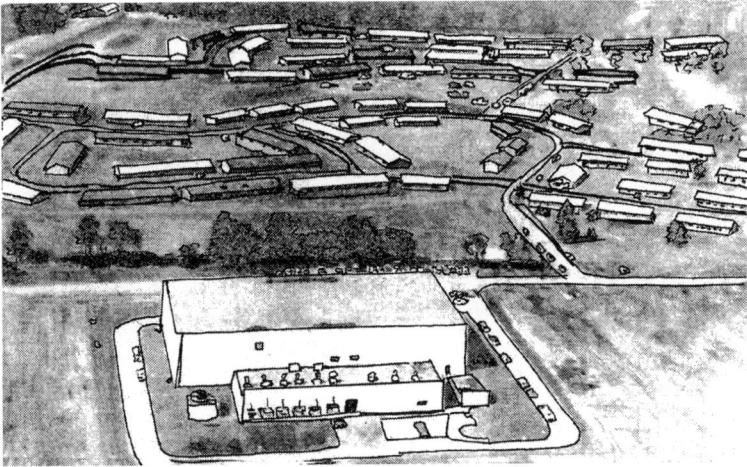

Democrat Herald

The Capehart housing for military officers and men with families. The SAGE building is three stories covering one acre in area.

On this site additional buildings were constructed including barracks, dining hall, officers' club, Base Exchange, dispensary, gymnasium, fire station, supply facilities and a headquarters building. On the north side of the station, streets and neighborhoods were created, and this Capehart housing later became Adair Meadows. The Air Force contracted with Keith Brown Company to build them. This Salem-based company shut down in

2008 as a result of the housing market crash. At their peak they operated 25 stores along the I-5 corridor.

In addition to the SAGE building and station facilities, construction of a CIM-10 BOMARC surface-to-air missile complex, from the Boeing Michigan Aeronautical Research Center and Nike, was begun in 1959 but was cancelled in March 1960, after the facility was 50% completed. The BOMARC missile site is now wooded and abandoned. Some concrete pads remain in the woods on Oregon State Forest Service land. SAGE operations continued until 1969.

The SAGE Direction Center at Adair was designated DC-13 Adair. Today, the SAGE building is a huge cement rectangle on Arnold Avenue, within the City of Adair Village city limits, and is privately owned.

2014 status of the 23 U.S. SAGE buildings:

DC-1: McGuire AFB, NJ	Military
DC-2: Stewart AFB, NY	Bell Atlantic (commercial)
DC-3/CC-1: Hancock Field, NY	Sutton Investment Corp. The Plowshare Complex
DC-4: Fort Lee AFS, VA	Military office space
DC-5: Topsham AFS, ME	Demolished August 1985
DC-6: Fort Custer, MI	Military
DC-7/CC-2: Truax Field, WI	Covance Labs
DC-8: Richards-Gebaur AFB, MO	Belton Tool and Machine

DC-9: Gunter AFB, AL	Offices
DC-10: Duluth IAP, MN	University of Minnesota Natural Resources Research Institute
DC-11: Grand Forks AFB, ND	Demolished
DC-12 / CC-3: McChord AFB, WA	Military
DC-13: Adair AFS, OR	Privately owned in the City of Adair Village
DC-14: K. I. Sawyer AFB, MI	Still an Air Force base
DC-15: Larson AFB, WA	Computer data-storage facility near Moses Lake, WA
DC-16: Stead AFB, NV	Was Desert Research Institute weather station. As of March 2000: military
DC-17: Norton AFB, CA	San Bernardino International Airport. SAGE building is a museum and television studio
DC-18: Beale AFB, CA	Military
DC-19/CC-4*: Minot AFB, ND	Offices for "Professional Results In Daily Endeavors" {PRIDE}
DC-20: Malmstrom AFB, MT	Military
DC-21: Luke AFB, AZ	Military offices
DC-22: Sioux City AFS, IA	A turkey processing plant
SCC-5: Hamilton AFB, CA	Demolished for housing development

In July 1969, the Air Force station land and buildings were returned as surplus property to the United States General Services Administration (GSA). Governor Tom McCall notified state agencies and educational institutions about the availability of the property. At that time OSU was building housing within Corvallis and preferred not to extend its campus to Adair. The GSA administrator spoke to the Oregon State Department of Rehabilitation and Vocational Services to see if they were interested, but nothing came of it. Linn-Benton Community College likewise refused the offer, preferring to remain located at Albany rather than Adair. In September of 1969, the Navy considered utilizing the property for a weather station. Hopes for this solution were dashed in December, when the Naval Headquarters in Monterey rejected the plan.

In February 1970, representatives from Benton and Linn counties, as well as from Monmouth, Salem and Portland organized the Willamette Valley Utilization Committee. They wanted to broaden the tax base in the area. Governor McCall allowed them time to make decisions about the property, which was referred to in the newspaper as a "14 carat opportunity." After a second two-day conference on the matter, John C. Kavanaugh of the GSA pushed the local communities for some hardcore objectives to get the Adair affair settled. Disposal of the housing units was a top priority because the state had inherited existing mortgages on that property, which amounted to $1.2 million. There was hope that someone would be able to make use of it. GSA wanted it sold as a single parcel and would not consider selling the houses to individual buyers.

 George E. (Eddie) Hoops was the Director of the Federal Property Assistance Program for the U. S. Department of Health, Education and Welfare (HEW), the department that served the U. S. General Services Administration. Eddie operated from the northwest offices, based in Seattle, Washington. He was in charge of the disposal of the Air Force property in the early 70's. He came to know the area and its people very well.

In April 1970, Eddie Hoops informed the United States International University (USIU) about the property available in Oregon. He had recently awarded this institution some surplus land around San Diego for their private college. USIU was a four-year liberal arts college that planned for 300 students the first year and

1,200 students within five years. It was founded as an affiliate of the Methodist Church, but broke their religious ties in 1967. They had campuses in London, Mexico, Kenya, Hawaii and Colorado, in addition to three in San Diego. There was support for the idea and the transfer of the deed for 204 acres and 36 buildings was made in September 1970.

But not everyone was in favor of the out of state, tax-free, California University receiving the property. Those most strongly opposed were some organizations supporting low-income and ethnic groups who were advocating for "the poor" in Oregon. The Council of the Poor had been organized after the Conference on the Poor had been held in Salem. This council planned to get a court action to freeze the transfer of the property to the university, even though the transfer had already occurred. They petitioned to "take back the land for the people." Idealistic plans and proposals for the use of the property for housing, educational purposes, a hospital and a vocational training center were made. The Mid-Valley Migrant Workers Group asked GSA and Health, Education and Welfare (HEW) to help them get the deed to the property. The Low Income Betterment and Rights Association of Salem (LIBRA) wanted housing and other facilities for low-income groups. Also involved were the Migrant Ministry and the Governor's Advisory Committee on Chicano Affairs. They threatened to picket the "turnover of the people's land" to someone outside of Oregon. These groups argued that Oregon did not need another expensive, private university only 12 miles from OSU.

USIU sent architects from San Diego to evaluate the buildings. They arrived at the same time that a group of protestors representing the poor in Oregon came to picket Adair, protesting the USIU transfer. One Chicano group called the Brown Berets showed up to keep peace at the entrance of Adair. The protests continued through October and resulted in the involvement of Benton County lawyers, Sheriff Jack Dolan, some FBI agents and at one point, the National Guard. The situation became more intense because violent demonstrations were happening all across the country. The political protests of the times were widespread. The Civil Rights Movement was at its most violent. In April 1968 Dr. Martin Luther King, Jr. had been assassinated, followed by Senator Robert Kennedy in June. In these contentious social times, protests were being staged for civil liberties and pro-feminism and against racism. Opposition was also increasing against the Vietnam War, as well as against biological and nuclear weapons, beginning the ecological movement.

The president of USIU, Mr. William C. Rust, was not comfortable with the local activist response at their newly acquired location. There had never been any political upset at any of their other university locations. The visiting architects were advised by USIU officials to "keep out of the way" because they didn't want to become engaged in this dispute.

The protesters' demands reached the office of Senator Mark Hatfield in Washington. Things remained in upheaval until the spring when protestors, antiwar groups, and the "poor" called for double protests at Adair. The persistent, though non-violent, controversy to "occupy Adair" was unsettling to USIU President Rust. He called for a probe of the situation.

Senator Hatfield called for a halt to the transfer and promised to look into it. In April 1971, USIU withdrew. The headline read, "USIU abandons Adair, President blames politics." The Governor began a new study on Adair. He made a tour of the property and invited 23 of the interested parties to come out and look around at the land and buildings.

Talks and planning sessions continued without much success. Police officials proposed Adair as a police academy, but federal authorities rejected this plan. Many old World War II cantonments around the nation had been reverted to National Guard training sites, and the Oregon National Guard pondered the possibility of acquiring the old station. The Air Guard general made a pitch for an air squadron to move in.

Gazette Times

The state-reverted property was deteriorating because of vandalism and neglect. GSA was putting out $8,000 a month for upkeep, but apparently road maintenance was low on the list.

Through the winter of 1972, panel discussions, hearings, committee meetings, and task force sessions continued but nothing could be decided because most of the interested groups didn't have sufficient financial resources to satisfy the GSA requirements. The abandoned station continued to deteriorate. The once utilitarian and tidy grounds were completely overgrown with tall grass and weeds.

Democrat Herald

Senator Hatfield (center with sunglasses) and Eddie Hoops (right) on the tour at the abandoned station with interested parties.

At this point, 24 different groups were interested in the surplus land and property. Numerous housing options were proposed, including a nursing home for disabled veterans, a family rehabilitation center, a non-profit vocational school, a senior citizen center, a drug rehabilitation center, a work-release farm for prison inmates, and a youth corrections facility. Other ideas posed were a statewide computer facility, a pesticide disposal site and a port facility for near-by US Route 20. Why? Because it's the longest road in the United States. Highway 20 begins at Newport, Oregon, and continues 3,365 miles across the continent to end in Boston, Massachusetts.

Gazette Times

The lonely spaces between abandoned Air Force station buildings in early spring. 1972.

In March 1972, the 150 Capehart living units and 66 acres were sold to real estate developer A. G. Proctor from Aurora, Colorado. He named the development Adair Meadows and sold homes to private individuals on the open market. He paid $2.5 million for the property, and the state was happy to alleviate the outstanding mortgage debt being paid by the taxpayers.

The State of Oregon had high standards of environmental quality and this, with the less than ideal location, discouraged potential industrial companies that may otherwise have been interested. After three years, GSA was losing patience with the lack of progress.

A drive-through wildlife zoo was considered in the E. E. Wilson Wildlife Area, but funding was not available. However, the Fish and Wildlife Department requested and received Firehouse Number 5, along with the former engineering building, which became their new regional office. Adair Village later obtained ownership of the firehouse, and it is now a grocery store and restaurant.

In August 1972, Benton County received the old Air Force station park area. First Lady Mrs. Pat Nixon attended the ceremonies to hand them the deed. It was valued at $80,000. The park included the old station tennis courts, skeet range, a small lake, hiking trails and other facilities, which became Adair County Park. Benton County also received an eight-acre parcel of land that included four incinerator buildings, two of which are now the Barracks, owned by Adair Village.

In November 1972, ten buildings on 14 acres were given to the Chicano Indian Study Center of Oregon (CISCO) for a live-in vocational and academic training center. Why? Because their pickets and protests were riding on the political coattails of a national drama. In Washington, D.C., Native American militants from the American Indian Movement (AIM) took over the Bureau of Indian Affairs Headquarters building to protest federal agency abuses. Elsewhere, Native American activist groups had gathered together to demand recognition of their rights. They intended to bring attention to Native American issues, including a demand for renewed negotiation of treaties, an enforcement of treaty rights and an improvement in living standards in the "red ghettos." On the eve of the 1972 presidential election and after the then-undetected Watergate break-in, a riot squad was called out and a paramilitary-style standoff ensued for five days. Months later, at Wounded Knee, South Dakota, AIM member Russell Means became famous for a 72-day standoff, where one Native American and two FBI men were killed in a shoot-out.

In comparison, the Adair takeover consisted of about 100 Native Americans and Chicanos who gathered in the gymnasium at the abandoned Adair Air Force station. This occupation lasted little over a day. It was small potatoes compared to what was happening elsewhere in the country. There was no violence here. In the end, the demonstrators achieved their goal. The U.S. General Services Administration promised to grant title to the property in Adair, which became the Chicano Indian Study Center of Oregon (CISCO).

Eddie Hoops supported this undertaking with additional funds and assistance. CISCO had big plans to meet the educational requirements of this endeavor, which included building a plant for making prefabricated housing components, as well as creating accredited college classes with OSU. This expansion to Adair from the CISCO headquarters in Portland was an ambitious venture. Regrettably, most of its capital came from federal grants that did not give allowance for repair or maintenance of buildings, which was mandatory under the federal deed. The costs involved were overwhelming. It survived for five years, but in spite of Eddie's $700,000 assistance from HEW, CISCO was forced to declare bankruptcy in 1977. When it left, 17 buildings and 24 acres were deeded to the Oregon and

SW Washington Laborers Training Trust for a construction laborer training school that had previously been operating at Camp Rilea, a National Guard Training Center in northwestern Oregon. The trust remained active in Adair Village until 2015. The land and buildings are now for sale. Things will change, again, with that property in Adair.

Gazette Times

Sheriff Jack Dolan talking with the Brown Berets in October 1972 at the takeover of the Adair gymnasium.

The City of Albany received the Adair water and sewer treatment plants in 1972 and reconnected the new occupants of the Adair area. Albany operated the plants until 1978, when they were reverted back to GSA.

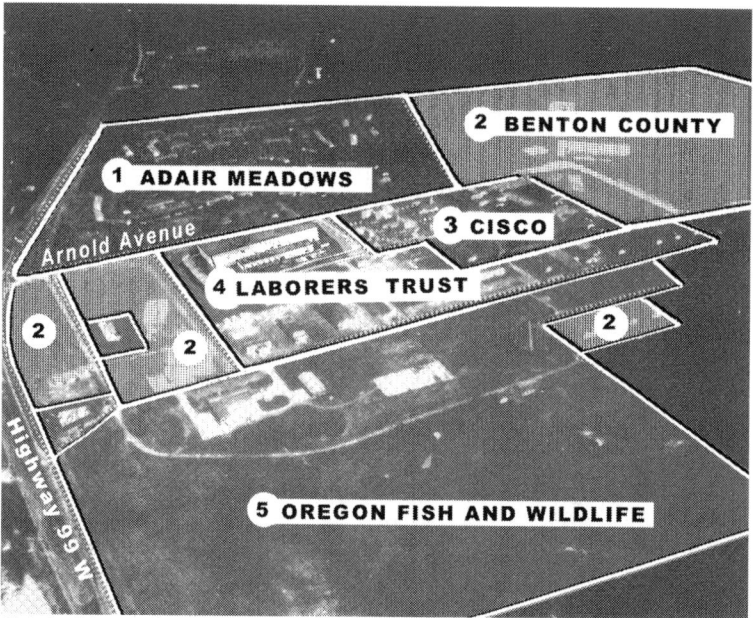

Original image from The Gazette Times modified by Delores Pollard

Allocation of Air Force station property in 1972:

1. Adair Meadows (sold to private ownership)
2. Benton County
3. CISCO
4. Oregon SW Washington Laborers Trust
5.Oregon State Fish and Wildlife

Of course, there have been many changes since this original disbursement of property.

Our dilemma is that we hate change and love it at the same time; what we really want is for things to remain the same but get better.

Sydney J Harris, an American journalist

Part 1:

Founding The City of Adair Village

Introducing the Women of the Adair Diary Project

Charline (Carr) King has played an important political role in the development of the city. Her desire to share her story led to the creation of this book. The history early years was written as a first person memoir, based on her previous written account of the adventures. Charline's last name was Carr when she first moved to Adair, but thirteen years after Bill Carr's death, she married Bob King, thus her name became Charline King. She is still living in her original house in Adair Village, is still devoted to protecting Adair Village and stays involved in city government even to this day.

Wanda Tobiassen, shares with Charline an "everlasting friendship" of 40+ years. She is the main collaborator with Charline on this history.

Judi Vedamuthu, the city archivist, was a genius of wit and generosity. She contributed much to the beginning city history and wrote the Forward.

Delores Pollard, an Adair Village resident since 1999, was the ghostwriter who came to know and love Adair through dedication to this work.

Chapter 1: Getting Here

It was July 15, 1973. My husband Bill Carr and I were moving our belongings from our apartment in Milwaukie, Oregon, to a place called Adair Meadows, halfway between Corvallis and Albany. It was a blistering hot day. We had endured the heat for the last hour and a half in a U-Haul truck with no air-conditioning. My first impression of the houses, duplexes and leftover military buildings, was less than encouraging. The lawns surrounding the houses and duplexes were scorched by the sun and lack of water. Only a few scraggly rose bushes decorated the front of our duplex. This was a desolate looking place!

Bill had recently earned an Associate Degree in Water and Wastewater Treatment from Linn-Benton Community College in Albany, Oregon. He had performed his on-the-job training for Albany and, to our delight, been hired for a full-time position as treatment plant operator. He wore out a car, driving from Albany back home to Milwaukie and we wanted a home closer to Albany. I gave notice to my employer in Portland. We gave notice to our landlord in Milwaukie. It was hard for me to leave Portland, to leave my family, my friends, not to speak of the theaters, musicals, and up-scale restaurants. We decided to give it a chance for one year and then move back to Portland if I so wished. I was excited to think about owning my own home. I had no idea what was in store for me.

Delores Pollard

Early view of Adair Meadows looking down Azalea Drive.

The former military base of Camp Adair was located only eight miles from Albany. Adair had been vacated in 1969 by the Air Force nearly four years earlier. A. G. Proctor had purchased the 1959 Air Force housing and was selling homes. John Fox Real Estate in Corvallis and Ransom and Smith Real Estate in Albany handled the sales. A retired electrician, Carroll Baker, temporarily lived in one of the Adair Meadows houses with his wife. He was hired to make sure all the appliances in the houses worked before people moved in. Proctor's representative, John Ankunding, and his family were also living temporarily in one of the houses. John had the task of selling all of the houses and duplexes before moving on to another development site owned by Proctor. They were here about a year. Because Bill Carr had worked with the Adair water plant, he got to know John Ankunding when hooking up the water to the houses. They liked each other and developed a friendship to the extent that we often played bridge with John and his wife.

There was a high demand for the purchase of these homes when put on the market, and all 60 duplexes sold in the first month. The Air Force station homes had been built after Congress passed the Capehart Housing Act in 1955. These homes differed from the earlier military family housing, which had been built under the Wherry Act, to keep the trained personnel near the bases after World War II. Capehart homes were built to larger specifications than the earlier Wherry units. The Capeharts each had a yard and were designed for single-family dwellings and duplexes. They were typical of a ranch-house style arranged into pleasant neighborhoods with consideration given for privacy and the preservation of the environment. Even though it was peacetime, the Cold War demanded that America remain on alert. The Air Force station at Adair was built around the SAGE building, which housed huge computers to process radar technology and BOMARC missile capabilities. Twenty-three of these SAGE radar stations were built across America and when the stations were closed, the Capehart housing units remained the property of the military. At the end of 1994, about 175,000 of these homes were still in existence. The Adair situation was unique in that it was isolated from any other military installation or base. Here the Capehart houses were released to the state and then sold into public hands.

Some far-sighted investors in our area took steps to buy up duplexes as investment properties. Wolfgang Dill bought nine duplexes, which were 18 future homes. At one time he was the manager of many of them. Eventually, he sold them but still managed some of them. Also, Dr. Robert Wilson, an allergist in Corvallis, bought five of them, which made ten living units. Some of these investors lived out of state and used the properties for rental income. These folks had no intention of living in the Adair area, but since the purchase price was reasonable and the structures in good condition, they seized the opportunity. Then there were people who, like us, wanted to buy a duplex for both a home and for rental income from the companion unit.

We were on a tight budget. The better rentals in Corvallis were too expensive for us and none were as nice as the one we had left behind in Milwaukie. I don't know who came up with the idea to apply for a duplex here, whether it was Bill or John, but we came down to Adair on a day off and because John and Carroll had the keys for their maintenance work, we looked around at some of the duplexes. They were heavenly, nice and roomy, compared to the apartments we had viewed, and they were affordable on Bill's salary. We could buy instead of rent! We knew we wanted a three bedroom duplex so we put our earnest money down, which amounted to $1,500 (in today's dollars that would equate to almost $8,000).

The way a person was able to buy a house from the realtors was to put earnest money down for a two-bedroom, three-bedroom or four-bedroom duplex or a single-family dwelling. The story was that all the names of all those who had paid their earnest money went into a hat. If your name was drawn out of the hat, you got a duplex or house. If it wasn't drawn, you were unable to purchase anything. You could not choose which duplex you would get. If you were lucky enough to have your name drawn out of the hat, the location of the home you got would be a surprise.

Our name was not drawn from the hat. Of course we were devastated. We were still living at our apartment in Milwaukie when John called and asked, "Did you get your duplex?" Bill said, "No, our name wasn't drawn." John said he was sorry to hear that. But he called us back the very next day and said, "You've got your duplex!" I will never know what strings he pulled but in some way he made sure that we got a duplex, and I have always been grateful to him. By the grace of God, our duplex was in a prime location. We paid $25,000 for the duplex at 162 NE Azalea. Our wonderful house was a three-bedroom duplex with a fireplace and garage, and nearly 1,200 square feet on each side. That doesn't seem like a lot of money now for all of that, but in 1973 dollars, it was equivalent to more than $130,000. A few years later, we were able to take advantage of an opportunity to buy an additional piece of land adjacent to us, a little over an acre, for $1,200.

Altogether, there were 60 duplexes, which made 120 living units and 30 single-family houses. Homeowners owned 39 of the 150 houses. The rest of them were rentals. There were 550 residents. This population remained the same for years.

Photo: Faye Abraham *at Adair Living History Presentation in 2012.*

Three original homeowners in Adair Village. From left: Charline (Carr) King, Betty Brown and Eugene Abraham.

More houses have been built in recent years. Plots have been divided and partitioned so it is much more complex now. When we first moved in, there was almost nobody here in the housing loops except Proctor's representatives and us. Every once in awhile in the evening, we would hear the rhythmic drumming from the nearby Sweathouse Lodge ceremonies. It was quiet and peaceful, even with the gray diggers. They were cute little squirrel-like animals that played in the streets because, of course, there were no cars around. They just made holes.

Let me tell you something about the Capehart house construction. I was impressed with those duplexes and how well they were designed and built by the Keith Brown Company in Salem. I will just speak about mine because they are all the same. We have added on and added on to the original part of the house that was built in 1959. The old part is structurally so much better than what we added later on. We are talking about 30 years earlier; building materials were better. They had true dimensional 2x4s, not the downsized versions we have today. And the 2x6 support beams that extend from the top of the roof out across the four foot eaves along the entire front and the back of the duplexes make an extended roof that shades the windows in the summers. The oak squares of the parquet floors are an inch and a half thick! It is hard to find those parquet pieces now.

The first thing we did after we moved to Adair was to install an air conditioner between the dining-living room area and the garage. Forty years later, that air conditioner is installed in our rental unit next door. Bill was one of those multi-talented people who could do anything, and he installed it himself. He made the first cut in the wall and discovered it was a double wall. Those walls are 6 inches thick! This was surprising. Even then, these houses were better constructed than other houses built in 1959. These were built to last. Isn't it true that some old things are so much better than what we can get now? This home was really a godsend, as far as Bill and I were concerned.

When we moved here, there were only a few fairly good-sized trees around and no shrubs. There were no flowers, except the three or four sickly rose bushes in the front of the duplexes, which were barely hanging on. To this day, it seems there are some units that still have those same rose bushes, and they are alive. We moved ours to the backyard when Bill and I started mowing, mowing, mowing and feeding, feeding, feeding and watering, watering, watering.

After all the houses were bought and people moved into this community, our quiet little place became a bustling neighborhood. The residents began improving their new homes, painting the exteriors, and building new fences. People planted flowers, shrubs and trees. We had to start nearly from scratch building our yards and gardens.

Charline's photo

Charline's house with the new hedge circa 1974.

I remember one afternoon in June of 1980, when a stranger rang my doorbell. He introduced himself by telling me he had been at Adair in the '50's, when it was the Air Force station. His job had been to plant a wide variety of ornamental trees. He said he had created a landscaper's dream here of manicured lawns, flowering azaleas and rhododendron shrubs. He called it a garden of perfection. When he left the service, he went back home to the East Coast. He now had returned to visit his creation, to see how it had thrived in twenty years. He thought he would see a wonderful thriving botanical wonder, but all that was left was a barren, parched mess. He was so disappointed that it was all gone. I told him what had happened here during the five years that the Adair area had been unoccupied, when some people saw it as a source for free landscape plants. They probably thought that if the government didn't want it, no one cared. Any plant small enough to carry away had been taken. All we had were new sapling trees and young bushes, recently planted by the new residents. I wish that landscaper could see the tall trees and the mature bushes that we have here now, forty years later.

It was uplifting to see the life and color in our new neighborhood, as things began to grow and bloom. A neighborhood garden club sprang up. It was mostly for women who were at home during the day. After we had all been here a year or so, an award went to the owners of the yard that showed the most improvement in the yard beautification contest. The prize was a $25 check, which meant something in those days. Bill and I entered the yard beautification contest, but we had gone to Portland the day the winner was selected. We came home to discover a sign in our front yard that read "First Place Winner." We were thrilled!

Chapter 2: Adair Meadows

Many people have definite ideas about the type of community they want to live in, but rarely do they have the opportunity to help create that community. Our chance was just beginning. I was fortunate to have that opportunity, to foster the strong sense of community that began to grow among those of us who lived here during those early years.

John Ankunding entered covenant documents for A. G. Proctor's Adair Meadows into public record in Benton County on May 10, 1973. Covenant 10 stated that in due course, a nonprofit corporation by the name of Adair Meadows Homeowners Association (HOA) would be formed. Eventually, we homeowners took advantage of this opportunity and held an election to formalize a Board of Directors. Mark Holliday was voted the president and his wife Dana was voted secretary. They lived on the corner of Laurel Drive where the three large redwood trees stand. Since I had some education in accounting and had worked with a C.P.A. while we lived in Milwaukie, my role as treasurer was a natural.

Delores Pollard

Putting a new waterline in the Kiddie Park in 2008.

We operated on a frugal budget. Our only income came from the annual dues paid by the homeowners: $30 for each single dwelling and $60 for a duplex. The total annual budget for our HOA was $4,800.

The Benton County Department of Outdoor Services and the Cement Mason Apprentice Training School helped us construct an outdoor basketball court up on the hill in the playground area between the two loops. As years went by, various other projects were completed. Many residents volunteered their ideas, their time, and their enthusiasm.

Some people moved here because there was no

limit on how many dogs they could have per household. Some actually came with five, six and seven dogs at a time and let them run loose. They ran in packs. They chased people. Dog control was an on-going issue. There was no leash law.

Dan Callahan, one of the residents who lived on Azalea Drive, was going to school at that time to become a veterinarian (as it turned out, he changed his mind and became a doctor, a podiatrist). His wife Polly was a nurse at Good Samaritan Hospital. He was coming home from school one day and a pack of dogs chased him. He ran to his front door with the dogs hot on his heels and later told us it was a blessing that, "For once in her life, Polly left the front door unlocked!" He got through it before those dogs could attack him. They did attack a little boy once who was badly injured.

The area around us was farmland, and the packs, both big dogs and little dogs, started going out into those fields killing sheep. The farmers were up in arms and killed a couple of the big dogs. We needed to address this. It was not safe to go for a walk because the dog packs were dangerous.

Lighting the streets at night was another issue. The streetlights were already there because the Air Force had put them in. There had been a few already turned on by the HOA. More were needed but we didn't have enough money to start adding up a big power bill.

The Adair Meadow's HOA met regularly and during those meetings the discussions more and more frequently revolved around the issue of our deteriorating streets. It was becoming a big problem. We needed help. We approached the Benton County Commissioners. Our streets were in an unincorporated area in Benton County and the commissioners had the responsibility to help us with repair and maintenance, but they refused to address our street problems, entirely. They said that the streets did not meet county standards. That was true, of course, because they had been built by the military. But they were the only streets we had and they were getting in worse and worse shape. We had no funds to repair them or to bring them up to any kind of standard.

Since the Benton County Commissioners were just not interested in assisting us, we realized that the only way we could get funding to repair the streets was to incorporate as our own city.

Judi

The feeling of Benton County and Corvallis towards Adair has been one of contempt... scorn. Those words may be too strong, but they looked down their noses at this area. I've always had the feeling that they thought they were a cut above.

Charline

That feeling may go back to the Army days. Some people in Corvallis and Polk County didn't like Camp Adair because it took away land, took away the rights of the people. It displaced people.

Judi

So there is that feeling that Adair is just not acceptable. I am not putting it very well, but the friction was there in our relationships with the surrounding communities and the government agencies.

Charline

There were other things that added to that stress. One thing was that CISCO was here and they had issues with violence and crime. We, the people living in Adair, know that is no longer the situation and it is an unfair perception of Adair Village now.

Chapter 3: Incorporation

Why not incorporate? We decided to go door to door to convince the residents in Adair Meadows that we should incorporate. Most people didn't care. They'd ask, "Why do that? Everything is fine." We told them we needed to incorporate because our streets were falling apart and we didn't have enough money to repair them.

We knew if we incorporated we would be eligible for a portion of the state's taxes: cigarette taxes, liquor taxes, the highway funds and all of that. We would also be able to apply for grants. It was a way of getting money to do what we needed to do, to upgrade and to run our little community.

Mark Holliday did the research for a lawyer and found Henry (Hank) Dickerson. We hired him to get the legal work done. I remember many meetings in Hank's office to draft the incorporation papers. He led us through the whole process. We, the Homeowners Association Board, were the ones that started and followed through with doing what needed to be done to take incorporation to a vote of the people.

Delores Pollard

This four-plex was part of the original Camp Adair hospital.

Benton County owned the clubhouse, and the 75-acre Adair Park, and wanted these to remain outside city limits. We didn't think too much about it, but later I thought that was a mistake. I'm not sure trying to persuade the county would have made any difference. We were so busy we didn't even try.

The former Air Force station properties are a patchwork of ownership, which have seen changes over time. The old Camp Adair hospital four-plex building, across the street from the Community Building, is now within the city limits, but the rest of that strip of land on both sides of it along William R. Carr Avenue, still belongs to the county, at this time. There is now talk of changes with some of that property.

Wanda's and my homes were both built in what is labeled on the old map as the First Addition. This lower loop of Columbia Avenue and Azalea Drive were designated that way on the Adair Meadows maps. According to the city documents, Adair Meadows was Laurel and Willamette loops. Some people call those Upper Loop and Lower Loop. One resident recalls that in the old days people referred to the Lower Loop as the Government Loop because so many council members lived down there. The upper loop was known as the Fireman Loop because so many volunteer firefighters lived there.

Many people still refer to Adair Village as Camp Adair. They don't realize that during the time it was Camp Adair there were no buildings here where the houses are now. The Air Force built them. So, when you look on the old maps and try to find the loops, what you see has no bearing to the loops at all, because they didn't exist. Laurel Drive was the road that came from the main part of the camp. By the way, some people call it the Air Force *base* but it was a *station*. It had no airstrip and it had no airplanes.

We contacted the county Records and Elections office and put the incorporation measure on the ballot that spring for the primary election of 1976. Again, we canvased from door to door, explaining the need for incorporation, informing the residents of the up-coming election, answering questions and in general trying to prepare our friends and neighbors so that they could make an educated vote.

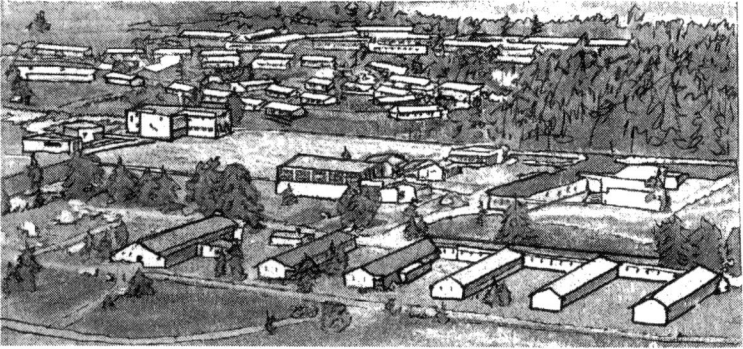

From a piece of photo originating from Benton County Historical Society.
Remaining covered walkways showing housing loops behind.

But something went wrong. There had been some confusion over the name of what we would call our proposed city. Somehow, during the printing of the ballots, a clerical error had occurred. We had filed papers that said it would be called The City of Adair Meadows but when we saw the ballots we noticed it had been filed in the office as The City of Adair *Village*. To make the change back to Adair Meadows at that point would have been too expensive, not only because the ballots would need to be re-printed, but also because we would miss the primary election date and would have to pay to set up a special election at full cost.

For the election, everyone who was a resident within the boundary of the proposed city received a ballot. But it wasn't precinct wide. If you owned a duplex or single-family dwelling but did not live in the area, then you could not vote. The people living here in Adair were the only ones who had voting rights. We had a discussion and asked, "Do we want to change the name back?" It had been Adair Meadows Homeowners Association who had started it all. We came to the conclusion that The City of Adair Village sounded good to us and that is how it appeared on the ballot.

I have a theory about why it is called Adair Village and not Adair Meadows. When the Camp Adair hospital complex was Adair Village Student Housing in 1948, they had their own homeowner's association That is when I lived here as a child. I think somebody in Corvallis didn't read Adair *Meadows,* but read Adair *Village,* because they made the map of the upper loop, it says Arnold Way, not Arnold Avenue. Arnold Way is in Corvallis, near the OSU campus. So, possibly somebody wasn't paying attention to details and they mixed up the old Adair Village Student Housing with Adair Meadows.

Judi

Chapter 4: Organizing

The vote was overwhelmingly in favor of the incorporation. We had won! Adair Village was now a legal city, the newest in the state of Oregon. We became the fourth city in Benton County along with Corvallis, Philomath and Monroe.

The City Council

The Adair HOA was still active, but was not legally prepared to run a city. Another election had to be held, this one to elect a five-member city council. There were nine candidates, so the ballot listed eight men and one woman: myself. The date for this important election was set for August 10, 1976.

The two council members, who received the highest number of votes, would serve for three years, the other two, for two years. In those days, the council elected its own mayor from the five members, to serve a four-year term. That was done for many years. Today, a mayor is chosen in a direct election to serve for two years.

We were the newest city in Oregon, and our council had the youngest members of any city council in the state. I was 36 years old when I was elected, and I was the senior member. Now, more than 40 years later, I am again the senior member of our city council.

The candidates for the first city council:

Sam Aikin, 28, 206 Cedar Lane. **ELECTED** with 71 votes. He was the only African American member and a graduate of West Texas State University. A resident of Adair Village for four months; a budget analyst for the State of Oregon, Sam believed he had the necessary budget and administrative skills to fulfill the duties of a councilman.

Samuel D. Aikin

Charline Carr, 36, 162 NE Azalea Drive. **ELECTED** with 55 votes. I thought my education in accounting at Clackamas Community College and my job experience as treasurer of the Adair Homeowners Association Board of Directors might aid me, if I were elected.

Charline Carr

Daniel E. Callahan

Dan Callahan, 24, 170 NE Azalea Drive. **ELECTED** with 54 votes. He was a pre-veterinary medicine major at Oregon State University (OSU) and worked at Town and Country Animal Clinic in Corvallis. An Adair resident for more than two years, Dan wanted to see our streets repaired, the dogs controlled, streetlights turned on and traffic control managed.

Michael Veach

Michael Veach, 26, 1214 NE Laurel Drive. **ELECTED** with 46 votes. He was a graduate from Umpqua Community College in civil engineering and worked for CH2M Hill in Corvallis. He felt he had a fair enough educational background that he could do the city some good.

Charles L. Phillips

Charles (Chuck) Phillips, 33, 180 NE Azalea Drive. **ELECTED** with 45 votes. An Adair resident for two years, he was a graduate of the Oregon College of Education in Monmouth. He was a correctional councilor for the work release center of Benton County. His three critical issues of interest included recreational facilities, traffic control and animal control.

The other candidates who ran but were not elected:

Michael Crouse

Michael Crouse, 27, 3130 Willamette, not elected, received 43 votes. An OSU graduate in Biology, he worked for the Environmental Protection Agency in Corvallis. A resident for two years, he supported recreational projects.

Bruce Koenig

Bruce Koenig, 25, 176 NE Azalea, not elected, received 27 votes. He trained as an airplane mechanic. In Adair for three years, he wanted to be involved in our community.

James M. Brinks

James Brinks, 32, 5228 NE Laurel Drive, not elected, received 12 votes. He graduated in botany/zoology from University of Montana. He hoped to keep the country atmosphere of the area.

Edward L. Bullard

Edward Bullard, 30, 3120 Willamette, not elected, received eight votes. He had a degree in social sciences from OSU, worked as a Christmas tree shearer and served in the Oregon National Guard. He believed it was important for Adair to grow slowly and not duplicate county laws.

Several days before our first council meeting (after the election and I knew I had been elected), I was visited by one of the other new council members. Chuck Phillips came to our house one evening and asked me if he nominated me for mayor, and if someone seconded it, and if it passed, would I accept that position? I told him that I did not know. It scared me. I had never been in an elected office and I had no idea how to run a city, particularly a brand new city. I told him that I had to think about it. I needed to talk to Bill about it, but he was at work. I told Chuck I would give him my answer the next day.

I thought plenty that night about being the mayor. There was no former mayor who could serve as a mentor to me. When I told Bill what Chuck had said, he knew this request indicated that the other council members had agreed that they would like me to be mayor. It was all but certain that his motion would be seconded and that it would pass. One other thing Chuck told me was to be sure to vote for myself! I was hesitant about voting for myself because I thought it would look like I had too much ego. But he insisted that I must vote for myself because we needed at least a three to two vote to succeed.

I explained it to Bill, "I don't know what to do. I just don't know." He knew I was apprehensive about it. Then he said, "Well, it's up to you. I'll support you either way. But, if you decide *not* to become mayor, I don't want to hear any complaints about the way this city is being run." He laughed as he said it and I did too. That helped me decide to tell Chuck that I would accept the nomination. I had become so involved in making this a better place to live that it just made sense. After all, how better to have input than to become the mayor of the new City of Adair Village? I was a second-year student in Humanities at Linn-Benton Community College in Albany at the time, and had been living in Adair Village for three years. My plan was to complete my four-year degree. It never happened. The world of politics sang her siren song to me and I followed.

On August 24, about two weeks following the election for city council, we held our first public meeting in the Benton County Clubhouse, which during Air Force occupation had been the Officer's Club. I was elected the first mayor of the City of Adair Village. The next day the headline in an article in Portland's *Oregonian* read *"Woman Named First Mayor."* The Corvallis *Gazette Times* headline proclaimed, "Adair Council Picks Carr as 1st Mayor." I had been elected by my fellow councilmen to lead this infant city in the right direction and I was a little more than nervous. None of the council members had ever been in this type of situation before. We were all brand new and starting out on a bright new adventure! In the newspapers I was quoted as saying I was going to need a lot of help from the council members. I have always felt some embarrassment about that because I felt it indicated a lack of confidence, and I knew I had a lot to learn. The newspapers made much of the election because I was not only the first mayor of Oregon's newest town, but I was also a woman!

The Commuter- Linn Benton Community College

Mayor Charline Carr with the City of Adair Village sign, 1978.

The seventies brought important changes for women in America. Oregon ratified the Equal Rights Amendment (ERA) in 1973. Women were taking more positions of authority in public service and I was one of them! The media's eyes were always on me and reported every action taken by our council, both wise actions and those that showed our lack of experience. Our first council was a solid, unified body. I could not have done as well without their support, assistance and affection. A strong bond was formed between us from the beginning.

City Auditor

With the council and mayor positions established, we got down to the real business of starting a city. Dan Callahan spoke with a well-respected public accountant in Corvallis, Louis Ramus, who agreed to work for Adair as our city auditor. Lou worked for us for many years until his failing health forced him to turn the job over to a younger accountant in his firm. He was very important to us at the start of our city because he helped to get our city budget established, which is a state requirement.

At our second city council meeting on September 16, 1976, Lou Ramus told us the Secretary of State would certify the recent census taken by Portland State

University by the end of the month, and after that we would receive funds from the state revenue taxes. The percentage would be based on the city's population.

Planning Commission

The council appointed seven people to our new Adair City Planning Commission. Mike Veach was the chairman of the Planning Commission, which included his wife Carla Veach, William Ross Hill, Mary (Phillips) Wright, Randall Rist, Mary Crouse and Jim Brinks. Mike Veach also headed a committee on street drainage problems.

City Recorder

Chuck Phillips took steps to find a city recorder. Lou said he would be available to help interview the possible applicants. They interviewed five candidates. The person would need to be bondable and would be covered by State Accident Insurance Fund (SAIF).

Wanda Tobiassen was one of the candidates we chose to interview. She had just moved to Adair with her husband Bill and their four boys. Chuck recommended that I interview her. She came to my house where I met her for the first time. I liked her immediately and told Chuck that I was impressed.

Wanda Tobiassen and her husband Bill.

Another woman had been interested, but said that Thursday, our chosen night for meetings, would not work for her. We wanted to keep meeting then, and since Wanda was qualified, lived in Adair Village and we liked her, she was duly appointed. Ironically, our meetings were changed to Wednesday only two weeks later. I guess Wanda was meant to be with us.

Our first order of business on the September 23, 1976 city council agenda was hiring our city recorder - for a probationary period. What a joke that was. Probationary period? She stayed for 24 years! Little did we know, at that first meeting, what a huge job it would turn out to be, in the coming years. Dan moved that

Wanda Tobiassen be hired for the job. The recommendation was approved by unanimous vote. She was hired for $3.00 an hour, to be increased to $3.50 after three months. Wanda used her home address for the city's business until a post office box became available from Corvallis. Sam Aikin began negotiations for acquiring a post office in Adair Village, but that hope has never been fulfilled. Forty years later we are still working toward getting our own zipcode.

One evening, Chuck Phillips came to my door looking for applicants for the job of city recorder. I was working part time for United Way of Benton County. I thought why not work two part time jobs, especially with one of them being here in the city? It was a natural choice for me.

Wanda

City Budget

We had to create a budget to start the city and to pay our city recorder. Lou took us through the steps. We formed a budget committee, which consisted of five members of the council and five appointees at large. Since there were only five of us on the council, we all had to be on it. Jim Brinks, Carla Veach, Tom Weygandt, Judy Dawson and Carol Roth were the appointees. It took 45 days to complete the process. We opened a bank account, authorized persons to sign checks at the bank and authorized investments of idle funds with the Oregon Local Investment Pool. Lou advised the purchase of a Fidelity Blanket Position Bond, ($378), to cover the authorized council members who signed checks and for liability insurance for each councilor in case a lawsuit was filed against us. By December, the council had joined the Public Employees Retirement System (PERS) to provide retirement coverage for the city employees and adopted the quarterly tax method for employment insurance for Wanda's position.

City Attorney

I had the easy job of finding a city attorney. Hank Dickerson, Jr. had guided us through the incorporation process when we were still Adair Meadows, and I asked him if he would be interested in working as our city attorney. We were delighted when he agreed. He was my right arm for the years I served as mayor. He held this position until he was elected as Benton County Circuit Court Judge several years later.

One day, in about 2010, when Wanda and I were having lunch at Shari's Restaurant, Hank walked by our booth. He stopped, turned around and said, "Are you two still together?" Thirty plus years later! He's a great guy. He was known for his honesty as a judge, and that has always been true of him. People called him "Honest Hank." The political endorsements described him as "Honest. Reliable. Dedicated." He was! He attended almost all of our early city council meetings.

Streets

Initially, we did not do much with the streets. We just fixed a few potholes and painted one side yellow in some places. The fire department told us we had to limit parking because the fire trucks could not get down our narrow streets with cars parked on both sides. The Air Force housing had two-way streets. So, we painted the curbs yellow on one side of each street and made some of them one-way through the loops.

We had Plan One and Plan Two. Plan One would remove parking from the east side of Cedar and a portion of Columbia Avenue. We would need nine gallons of paint, at $3.75 a gallon, and one stop sign that would cost $13.50. Plan Two would permit parking on both the east and west sides of Cedar but only in designated areas. That plan needed six gallons of paint, four "No Parking" signs, four posts and one stop sign. Chuck moved that the first plan be adopted. The motion passed and some of the councilmembers got to work, painting curbs yellow and planting stop signs.

Delores Pollard

Looking southeast up Azalea Drive. A two way street in 1976.

Eventually, we applied for and received grant money to fix the streets. We contracted with Morse Bros. Building and Supply Inc. to do the work on intersections at Laurel and Willamette, Columbia and Cedar, and Azalea west of Cedar. The cost was $462 (in todays dollars; $1,896).

> **Charline** In 2012, Benton County filled the hole in the street on the corner of Azalea and Columbia They agreed to come out if they were in the area, and soon they arrived. We paid them $5,000 for that street repair. They did a great job in a timely manner.

Meeting Places

Our meetings were taken up with reports on the assignments that our respective council members had assumed. Almost everything was reported in the newspaper. Reporter Bill Monroe did a lot of writing about Adair Village for *The Gazette Times* in Corvallis. I remember one time, before we had an official place to meet, Bill wrote that we were "meeting among the crumbs and jams."

> **Wanda** I remember once in the middle of a city council meeting at CISCO cafeteria, two little puppies came in chasing each other, scampering under the tables, around and around our feet and then right back outside.

We met in so many different places. We frequently even met at my dining room table, especially for emergency meetings. We really needed a building to meet in. The lack of a fixed location made it hard, especially for Wanda with the files and papers and tape recordings for transcription of the meetings minutes, which were piling up in her home.

I think the worst place we ever met, and it was probably illegal, really, was an upstairs room in the Blockhouse. That is what many of us still call the old Air Force SAGE building, now the ACC Building.

That Blockhouse is a scary building, a ghost building in a way, deep, and dark. Going into that huge, huge building is an experience all its own. It is spooky and anyone who has been there will agree. We would go in at night, way up the stairs and we were the only people there. That was before the windows were put in. I feel that never should have been done. It destroyed the historical value. That building was made to withstand anything but a direct hit from an atomic bomb. It compromised the security.

The building could be used to house many people in emergencies, since it is three stories high and covers an acre per floor! The folks of Adair Village could fit in it if necessary and all of the surrounding communities, too. Now it is privately owned. When it was for sale, the asking price was too high for the city to purchase. We met in the Blockhouse, but only three or four times, because we had to have a place the public could access. If you were handicapped, it would be a hardship to get up all those steep steps. It was a safety issue, too. You have to be able to get out fast if something happens. So, we went back to meeting at my dining room table.

Delores Pollard

The former Portland Air Defense Wing Headquarters. Before completion, operations were conducted from a building loaned by Oregon State Game Commission, now Fish and Wildlife.

We met in the cafeteria and conference room of CISCO (Chicano and Indian Study Center of Oregon) for the first six months. When they left, we met for the next six months in the Sweathouse Lodge cafeteria. Sweathouse Lodge was an extremely successful private alcohol detox program for Native American males. It had a high success rate. It was one of a few facilities in America that offered sweat lodge purification ceremonies for Native Americans. The facility housed 30 or 40 persons. After Sweathouse Lodge left in 1979, the Santiam Christian School moved in and opened with 55 students. We were happy to see something come that would grow and be an asset to the city.

Delores Pollard

Sweathouse Lodge allowed the public to visit its wigwams.

If you looked at the members of our city council and the budget committee, you would see that the members of the planning commission were married to people on the city council, or to people on the budget committee, and so forth. We were all in this together. These people were interested in what was happening here and were willing to serve on those committees. The bottom line was that a very small group of us were truly devoted to making Adair Village a city, committed to seeing it progress, by serving on the necessary key committees. We needed strict control on animals. We needed our streets fixed, but my bigger vision for the future was to see the city beautified and upgraded. I also hoped for a small grocery store and a child daycare center for working families.

We need more people and more money for our city to grow. It is not easy to find people who will commit themselves to participation in the city government. Folks get involved sometimes only for the fulfillment of a personal agenda, not really with a commitment to the city as a whole. Others are committed, but their life circumstances change and they move away. We had a very large renter population in the early days of Adair Village. We had no zero lot line zoning then, and many people came, but did not buy the homes and stay. Many people did not take us seriously as a city. People were here and then they were gone.

In 1973 the properties along Arnold Avenue and parts of Laurel Drive were empty fields. Eventually, these lots were filled.

We had to handle all sorts of problems. We had what we called the Midnight Moves. People would move out without giving any notice, leaving water, sewer, electric, and many other bills unpaid. One night, for example, on Azalea Drive, the renters moved without notice but they left something behind. And nobody knew it until the neighbors informed us about a big racket coming from inside an empty unit. We investigated and found there were some sheep in the dining room! They had been in there for three or four days without food or water. They finally started bellowing and the city responded. Of course, that duplex was trashed. The owner had to replace the entire parquet flooring. You can imagine how thrilled he was.

Hiring helpful professionals proved to be one of the most positive early decisions our young and inexperienced city council made. We surrounded ourselves with the right people: Hank Dickerson, Lou Ramus, and Don Driscoll, our first city planner. We might have been inexperienced, but the people we hired on contract, even though they worked part-time, were very experienced. Whether it was law, planning, financing, or anything else we needed, we sought out top-notch advisors. I remember that after we hired Hank, he and I talked on the phone every day during those first few months. I was learning, learning, and learning, and I had to learn fast. Wanda, too, was constantly on the phone with our accountant. We were serious about learning all we could from the smartest people we could find. In those crucial first years our lawyer and our auditor, one or both, attended almost every meeting. They advised us on the legal steps to take to manage a city. These helpful mentors whole-heartedly immersed themselves in the genesis of the city and stuck with us through thick and thin.

Charline

Samuel Aikin and his wife Betty lived kitty-corner from Bill and me. They were not in the HOA because they were renters, not homeowners. However, they were very enthusiastic about the incorporation. Sam had his heart set on becoming our first mayor. However, his interest had nothing to do with enhancing our area. He told us he thought that becoming mayor would look good on his resume. That didn't sit well with any of us. We were looking at the long-term future. He was not really interested in it the same way that we were.

After the council elected me as mayor, Sam quickly lost interest in any city business. He stopped attending meetings. This was stressful because we needed everybody on board. Every council position was important, because we were just beginning to establish the city. We had to declare his position vacant, and the council appointed Michele Ryker to complete Sam's term.

Chapter 5: Starting Our City

In the fall of 1976, we plunged eagerly into the adventure of starting our city. There was much to be done. Wanda and I worked hand-in-glove in those early days. We were in contact every day, by telephone or in person. There were no days off, but it was a fun time for all of us as we worked to make sure the city was started on a solid foundation.

There had to be a great deal of communication between members in between meetings, to keep us on track. More than two council members getting together would have been a violation of Oregon's public meeting laws. Three councilors together made a quorum, and that meeting would have had to be announced to the public in the newspapers. As mayor, I met separately with each of them in order to convey and glean information without violating that law. Much of our communication and planning happened by telephone, just two of us talking, which was allowed.

We tried to think of all that needed to be done. Our resolutions were written, often re-written, voted on and passed by the council. Our book on Roberts Rules of Order was used until we knew it by heart. We made community contacts under the supervision of our advisors with various supportive organizations.

Judi

There are many steps to take to make a new city that are not apparent from the outside. You guys were just racing to get so many things done. You succeeded in realizing many of the ideas that you had in the beginning. The ones that are still not manifested today are good ideas for the future community.

Council of Governments

We invited Bill Hageman, the Executive Director of the Council of Governments (COG), to speak at a city council meeting. We eventually paid the dues and became a member of that group. COG served as a clearing-house for federal grant money and helped us with such things as long range planning of water and land use. The Comprehensive Education and Training Act (CETA) was an offshoot program of COG, which helped the city with several construction projects over the years.

League of Oregon Cities

We contacted The League of Oregon Cities (LOC), who explained the advantage of joining their organization in order to learn about the newly devised planning requirements of the Oregon Land Conservation and Development Commission (LCDC). The LCDC helps cities develop state mandated planning and zoning ordinances. We contacted Marvin Gloege, then the Linn-Benton Planning Coordinator, who agreed to help our planning commission develop a comprehensive plan for Adair Village and to start grant applications.

Law Enforcement

We knew we needed some way to guarantee public safety in our city. We invited John Cromly, the mayor of Sodaville, a small Linn County city incorporated in 1880, to speak about the problems they had encountered in setting up a volunteer police force. Sam Aikin contacted John C. Williams and Robert Fisher of the Oregon State Police about getting a state police officer to patrol the city. In December, Frank Dieu, of the Benton County Sheriff's Department, spoke to the city council concerning law enforcement protection in Adair Village. Frank said that at that time Adair Village could not contract with Benton County for law enforcement protection, but that the county would give aid whenever possible. There were patrols coming through, but not on a regular basis.

The Benton County sheriff's department was willing to answer 911 calls. A call would be routed to a call center first, and then relayed to the sheriff's department. A deputy or someone would make a decision as to the importance of the call, whether it involved property damage, endangerment to a person, a life or death emergency, or something else. If it looked like the response could be put off until the next day, they would wait until then. There is really no absolute prevention of crime. The police have to wait until a crime has been committed before they can act.

Health Services

The Benton County Health Department was able to provide us with limited health services including inoculations and an x-ray unit. Even today in Adair Village we have no health center, but it remains something we want to create as our city grows. In 1976, Bill Hill was the coordinator of social services for CISCO. We participated with them for Swine flu inoculations and also for a low-income dental clinic at school in Corvallis.

The Adair Rural Fire District

By 1976, The Adair Rural Fire District had been operating for three years, and Dennis Haney was the fire chief. Now he is the area Fire Marshal and has served in that capacity for a number of years. Assistant Fire Chief Chuck Harris spoke to our council about emergency medical training and everyone on the city council received that training. We still had a homeowners association up until 1981 when it was disbanded, but our HOA helped fund some of the safety and emergency equipment: a Life Pack for $6,000 and a portable radio for $1,500, for the fire district.

Dog Control

At long last, in the fall of 1976, we began to address the dog control issue in the community. We had to write an ordinance for this. It was the first one we wrote as a city council. We learned that some ordinances must be filed with the State of Oregon, while others that deal with certain specific laws must be filed with the county or the city. Crafting the ordinance was more complicated than we imagined. We met with the Benton County dog control officer about the requirements for an animal control officer.

In the summer of 1977, Hank wrote a letter saying there were discrepancies that "may place duties on the county that they may not be willing to fulfill." In enforcement cases where persons plead not guilty, the district attorney would no longer represent us. The cases were taking up too much of the district attorney's time and finances.

 Charline

We had to buy Worker's Compensation insurance for any animal control officer. One officer filed a complaint for an "on the job" injury. Consequently, that claim went against our insurance record and increased our premium. As it turned out, the officer was not injured in the course of her job. I know that because an eyewitness told me what really happened. The injury occurred in the officer's own backyard. But she put the responsibility on the city. That was dishonest. I did not pursue the matter because by the time I found out the claim was already filed.

We had to rewrite that ordinance many times. In June of 1979 the county commissioners signed a final contract. In the end it was agreed that Benton County District Court would process our cases, but we had to pay our own lawyer to prosecute them. There were many amendments to the ordinance. It was not simple. Completing it was a long, drawn-out process.

Delores Pollard

Dog walking is a common sight at Adair Pond.

Public Services

Pacific Northwest Bell and Consumers Power Inc. allowed us to receive a small portion of the local telephone and power bills. There was an existing cable system left behind from the old Air Force station, which we used to connect to television.

Charline

We have tried and tried to work with Oregon Department of Transportation to do something about the Frontage road. Really, what we want is for the State to bring it up to some kind of maintenance or grade. It has potholes and the asphalt is broken out in places. We want them to fix it up and then give it to the city. We don't want something that has to be completely rebuilt. ODOT has pretty much just ignored it. Ever since I have been back on the Council, which has been eight years, we have been trying to get that considered. I think it has totally fallen through the cracks. Literally.

Judi

You could have it closed, but you have to get an agreement from the people who use it further to the north, who have access to their property through there.

We contracted for garbage pick-up service with the privately owned Corvallis Disposal Company. Some people still take their garbage up to Coffin Butte landfill. Others use Frontage Road and throw their garbage in the ditches. We don't like that a bit.

The Air Force straightened Highway 99W in 1960. It eliminated several miles of curvy road through the foothills. It started outside of Lewisburg and ended at the old Camp Adair cantonment entrance. The Frontage Road is a small loop at the northeast end that was left in place when the new Highway 99W took out a mature orchard on the Hardenbrook property west of the highway. On the southeast end, the new highway split farmland belonging to Charlie Fox at the time. Anderson's Blueberry production was established in 1982 between the new highway and the old highway, which is now called Arboretum Road.

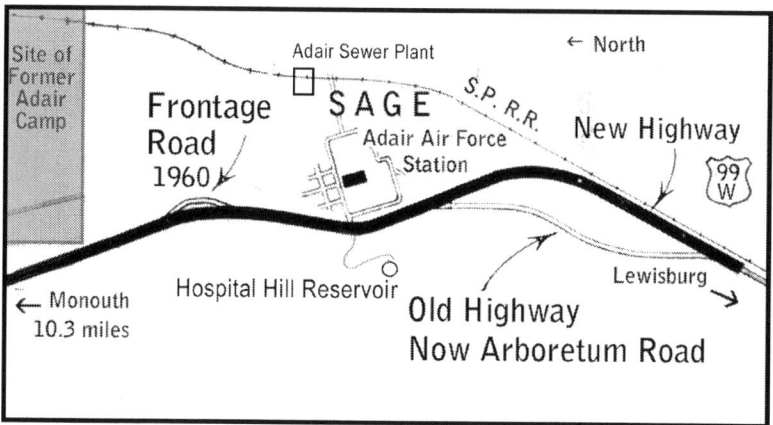

Land Use Plan

In 1973 the State of Oregon adopted Senate Bill 100. That legislation required every city to create a comprehensive land-use plan. This was new territory for us at the time, but we met the deadline the state set. Our city's urban growth boundary decisions were part of this, and as we grow, the Adair Village comprehensive plan is periodically updated.

In 1976, the Planning Commission asked the city council to pass a resolution establishing a moratorium on building in Adair Village. We wanted to preserve 20 acres of open space within the city until we could complete our land-use plan.

From the beginning of Adair Village, we had Don Driscoll as the city planner. He helped us create our city charter and our zoning ordinance. The land use development code had to be created, as well. The only time that he was not the city planner was when Jim Minard was our city administrator. Minard fired Don and became both the administrator and the city planner. I felt that decision was a big mistake. We hired Don back when Minard left the position in 2007. Don is still our city planner at this time in 2016.

ADAIR VILLAGE

KIWI LN.
NEWTON RD
NORTON RD
HYACINTH
HIBISCUS TER.
BARBERRY
DAPHNE CT.
AZALEA DR.
CEDAR
COLUMBIA AVE.
CAMDEN
KIDDIE PARK
CHURCH
WILLAMETTE AVE.
ServPro
ADAIR COUNTY PARK
SEWAGE TREATMENT PLANT
N.W. ARNOLD AVE.
EBONY
ARNOLD AVE.
Original UGB Boundary
COUNTY PARK
SAGE
SANTIAM CHRISTIAN SCHOOL
FIRE DEPT.
LABORERS TRUST
BIRCH LANE
N.W. ARNOLD AVE.
VANDENBERG AVE.
OREGON DEPARTMENT OF FISH AND WILDLIFE
PURPLE VETCH
ADAIR POND
RYALS AVE.
PORTLAND
WEST
NEW UGB BOUNDARY
UGB EXPANSION AREA 127.5 ACRES
US HIGHWAY 99W

0   1000   2000

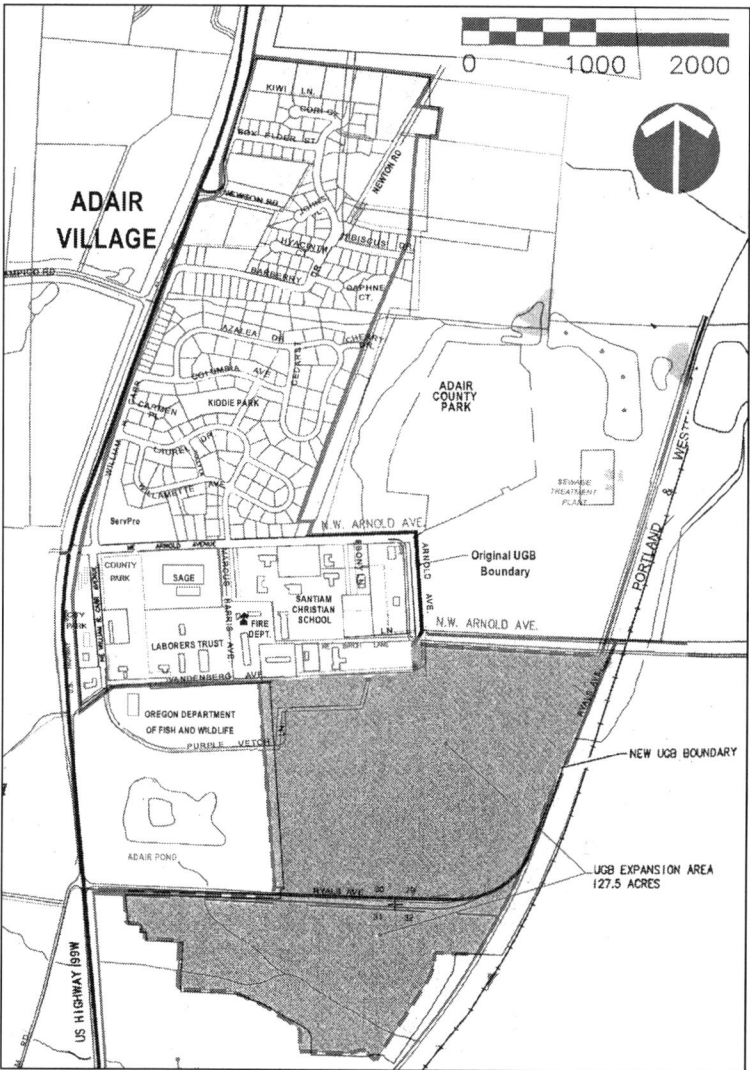

Delores Pollard

Adair Village has changed quite a bit since 1973. This
map shows the rectangle of the old Air Force station in
the center, with the Adair Meadows housing just north
of it. Further north is the first housing expansion. The
gray area at the bottom shows the expanded urban
growth boundary.

Projects

Laborers Trust built our bus shelters.

The HOA built some school bus shelters in 1976, but we really needed more. We wrote permission letters to the owners of the houses where the bus stops would be built. Only one resident refused. The Laborers School built the new ones for us and repaired the original ones.

Delores	You had vandalism damage to the bus shelters?
Wanda	Well, things don't change.
Charline	There for awhile, we had parents going to the bus stops with their kids in order to stop that kind of vandalism.

Judi

You do things to make it nice for people, and somebody comes along and stomps all over it and after awhile you begin to ask, "Why bother?" We had to fix that water fountain again for the Summer Program this year. It was an emergency fix. You can't have people in a place where there is no water for them.

Charline

That has always puzzled me as to what pleasure somebody gets from ruining something that is useful, or pretty.

Delores

If they had been part of solving the problems that needed to be solved, they would appreciate how much work it is to make something good.

Judi

Or if they helped build it they would have skin in the game.

Delores

Yes, with involvement comes pride. If people feel it is their own they maybe appreciate it. But when it is just given, for some people it becomes something to destroy, to exert power over, and perhaps to get a feeling of control over something or somebody in their lives.

In 1976, resident Lorraine Ruff headed a street beautification committee. Some crab apple trees were planted along Columbia Avenue. Each tree was worth about $8.50 (around $45 today). Two of them just disappeared in the night. Someone dug them up and packed straw into the holes.

Delores Pollard

The old church property was sold in 2015. Change is coming.

We had a big problem controlling the weeds, both in people's yards and Proctor's lands. We adopted a city ordinance for cutting the grass at six inches, then again, rewrote it later at ten inches. We sent a letter to Mr. Proctor about this but he did not answer us. The city finally hired someone to mow it and keep it neat.

Gazette Times

Overgrown lot at the Air Force station telephone building on Arnold Avenue in 1976.

City Hall

William Chapman, Benton County park director, spoke on the possibility of using the old procurement building, located near 99W, as a community center. Applications for a grant to finance the repairs were due January 1, 1977. We applied right away because an official city needs to have an official place to meet. By October 1978, we had our own.

Charline	Six months after we incorporated, the city started paying the power bill for streetlights. Before that it was the homeowners association that paid for that service to the community.
Judi	It is funny how we take things for granted, like streetlights. Who ever thinks about who is paying for them?
Charline	But let me tell you, when it is dark, dark, dark out there, streetlights become a big priority.

Lawyers

In the beginning we had our attorney who guided us on nearly every aspect of how to legally become a city. Things were done quickly and efficiently. Since Hank moved on, there have been several attorneys on contract with the city. Because of the cost, the attorney attends only those meetings requested by the city council. Occasionally, if it happened that there is something controversial or a significant legal question, we have an executive session on our regular council meeting agenda and have our lawyer there in person or on speakerphone. When a citizen filed lawsuits against the city, every ordinance and resolution had to go through the city attorney. Even the most routine, mundane things had to have his legal opinion. It really slowed things down. All the citizens had to pay for this service. It was a complete waste of time and money.

The lawsuit said we were in violation of our city charter because our city administrator, police chief and public works director, all of whom were appointed to executive positions, had to live within the city limits of Adair Village. We talked in great length with our city attorney about the issue, and his legal opinion was that our charter did not require these executives to live in the city. It gave us the *option* of doing so, but did not r*equire* us to do so. The citizen who brought the lawsuit interpreted it in a different way. The lawsuits were eventually dropped.

Public Works

The Adair Village water and sewer services came from the old Camp Adair military facilities. The water treatment plant is located several miles west of Albany. We had concerns about the security of our water supply coming from Albany. We appointed a committee in March of 1977 to meet with Albany officials to discuss matters. Dan said he would like to see the water rates lowered and a specific amount of water allocated to each household. We wanted to know: What percentage of their water revenues came from Adair Village? What was the cost of maintaining the Adair water plant? Most importantly, we wanted to know what obligation the city of Albany had to supply water to Adair Village. The answers were vague, but we were assured that our water supply was plentiful. However, we were advised to be conservative with it. They were committed to supplying Adair with water and sewer service, but they said that the system was not self-supportive. We didn't know what that meant, but we eventually found out.

Albany charged a fairly good price, but was considering a rate increase. Albany had replaced some water lines along Azalea Drive with PVC piping and had put in some new meters. As far as Albany was concerned, they were taking care of us and we had nothing to worry about. We wanted to present ourselves to them as an incorporated city, not just as private individuals from Adair Meadows. Albany's response was enough for us to table the issues to the year's end. But in January of 1978, the issue of our water supply engulfed our regular city business, and swept us into a flood of controversy that lasted nearly two years.

Part 2:
All About
The Water
1978

Chapter 6: First Water Crisis

In late January of 1978 we received a notice from Albany that our water service would be shut off in one week! We attended an Albany City Council emergency meeting on water service. It was packed with angry people worried about their water supply. We had no idea what was really going on. We'd been busy creating our city during the last 14 months and had not gotten back to Albany with questions about water and sewer contracts for the incorporated city, as we had planned after meeting with them the spring before. Now, Albany had passed a resolution to return the plants to the federal agency, the Health Education and Welfare Department (HEW). We were very concerned about what might happen if those services were shut off! As city officials we had to take action.

We learned that Albany was demanding that the government take the Adair water plant back. We had recently seen CISCO lose their federal property in the spring of 1977, so we knew it could happen. We learned that shutting down the Adair water plant would affect approximately 800 people. Over 500 of those people lived in Adair Village. We felt this was a threat.

Gazette Times

Jim Ableman, Charline and Wanda at our first emergency council meeting in Charline's dining room in January 1978.

Somebody brought up the fact that legally Albany would have to operate for a year after giving notice of a shut off. That stipulation held true only for a few of the outlying customers who had signed delayed annexation agreements with the city of Albany, and it didn't apply to us since we had no legal agreements. We felt vulnerable. We considered seeking a court injunction to force Albany to keep the Adair water plant running for Adair Village and for those other neighboring residences on the Adair water system.

Immediately after attending the meeting in Albany, we called our first emergency council meeting to brainstorm about it together. It took place at my dining room table. A newspaper reporter had followed us home, which was okay because city council meetings are public events. The next day the *Gazette Times* newspaper headlines read: "Adair's council miffed."

Gazette Times

Worried councilmembers: Michele Ryker, Dan Callahan and Chuck Phillips at the emergency meeting.

We didn't understand what was going on, but we knew North Albany was involved somehow, and so were the state, county and federal governments, but how and why? We needed to get that information.

North Albany was an unincorporated community in northeast Benton County, across the Willamette River from Albany, which is in Linn County. Councilman Chuck Phillips attended the next meeting of the North Albany Service District Advisory Board, and he brought back the story about what was happening. North Albany was protesting Albany water service policies requiring annexation for services. They started the process of unifying their 13 water districts to be able to legally contract for water service from someone, either from Albany's Adair water plant, or from Pacific Power and Light Company (PP&L).

The Adair water and sewer plants and systems had been officially transferred to Albany in 1972 under the requirement that they provide sewer service to North Albany within 24 months and potable water as soon as possible after that without attaching conditions. For the last six years, Albany had owned and operated the plants. Sewer lines had been built under the bridge across the river to North Albany and a new state of the art sewer plant had been built to solve Albany's sewer problems, but Albany had not yet gotten around to solving the potable water problem for North Albany, which was a stipulation of their federal quitclaim deed.

New housing developments were springing up in North Albany, creating more homes, wells and septic tanks. The problem was that the winter rains were causing cross-contamination in the drinking water from the septic system drainage on the slopes of North Albany. Water samples showed traces of human and animal waste in the well water in seven of the 13 water districts when it rained. This was not a new problem. The Federal Environmental Protection Agency (EPA) put pressure on the State Board of Health to resolve the public health hazard. North Albany had 60 days, at the beginning of January 1978, to find a solution or to be forced to annex into the city of Albany. Nobody wanted forced annexation. But contaminated wells? You don't turn your back on that for long!

The struggle between Albany and the people of North Albany over water service had culminated in bad feelings on both sides. Albany's questionable demand of signed delayed annexation agreements and the water pricing policy that went along with them was offensive to many North Albany residents. Albany offered one rate for people who signed their annexation agreement and doubled the rate for those who refused to sign. North Albany residents complained to Senator Hatfield who then requested HEW's help, particularly of Eddie

Hoops, whom he had worked with on the Adair property allocations in the past, to investigate Albany to see if they were complying with their deed.

Eddie was the watchdog over surplus government properties. The Adair water plant with its delivery system was one of these. Eddie had met with the Albany officials in late December about Senator Hatfield's concern over Albany's requirement of signed delayed annexation agreements in return for water service to North Albany. At that time, Eddie decided that Albany was complying fully with the terms of their deed. But then something happened that changed his mind.

Some North Albany residents met with Eddie and told him that they believed Albany's deed stated that no conditions would be required for the sale of water from the Adair water plant. The forced delayed-annexation agreements were a condition that was illegal. Copies of the deed that so stated had been anonymously passed out in the community, to the chagrin of Albany officials. Sometimes people do things under pressure that they normally wouldn't do. This was the 70's and the atmosphere of the free speech movement was strong in the undercurrent of the political attitudes of the times. Democracy was very alive and well. Many people were proactive and when problems arose, they organized, voiced their opinions and marched for their rights.

The North Albany protestors, led by resident Clacia Young, spoke to Eddie Hoops. These protestors were instrumental in changing Eddie's mind about Albany's state of compliance. Young told him the protestors felt that Albany was using the water system and the area's public health problem as a political club to force the area into annexation on the city's terms. The watchdog in Eddie perked up his ears. He heard information that changed his decision. He wrote a letter to Albany City Manager Hugh Hull saying that Albany was violating the stipulations of their deed, and that they were *not* in compliance with their quitclaim deed, after all. Eddie said he was wrong to tell them that their delayed annexation policies were okay. The bottom line was that they *could not* require signed annexation agreements in exchange for water service. They had to provide water without these conditions.

Eddie gave Albany a week, until Feb 1, to respond. The North Albany Service District Advisory Board wanted the water plant reverted from Albany, thinking perhaps they could run the plant themselves for their projected 7,000 residents.

North Albany protestors picket the closed meeting of the Albany City Council with signs that read, "Help HEW."

The North Albany water district had organized a picket line in front of the Albany courthouse. They asked public officials to get involved. They wanted Eddie and HEW to force Albany to fulfill its deed to deliver water without annexation demands or else to revert the plant from Albany.

The Albany City Council responded that they *were in compliance* with the deed and responded on February 2, telling Eddie to "TAKE BACK THE PLANTS!" Albany was determined to keep their city's local laws about delayed annexations. After all, it had been their policy for years.

Democrat Herald

Albany Mayor Roche and Albany City Attorney Merle Long in conference at a city council meeting in Albany.

All of us who were receiving water service from the Adair water plant were warned that within a week that plant would be shut down!

We were determined to work together to protect our city, and to keep our rates as low as possible. Additionally, Mr. McDougal from the Oregon State Fire Marshal's Office informed us that an uncertain water supply would affect the rating they gave Adair Village, which would consequently raise all homeowner's insurance rates. That is when we got involved in the fray. We voiced our concerns to Eddie Hoops and wrote letters to Senators Mark Hatfield and Bob Packwood. We had no guarantee of consistent service. We were only informed about the operation of the water plant every two weeks, when Albany's City Council met.

Forced annexation: the State of Oregon could legally force North Albany to become a part of Albany to deal with the recurring water contamination issue.

Delayed annexation: Albany could decide when to choose annexation and could charge higher water rates to those customers who did not sign a waiver that would allow them to be annexed to Albany sometime in the future. Delayed annexation would give the city time to meet the financial needs of annexation on their own terms.

The media became involved in the water controversy for a number of reasons. The first was because there were so many people involved in the issue. The Adair water controversy spanned local, county, state and federal responsibilities. The second reason was that the City of Adair Village was so new. The media was still watching us closely. The third was Eddie Hoops' flamboyant personality. The media called him a newspaper reporter's dream with his forthright, consistent, and blunt approach to the issues. He verbally expressed himself in a dramatic way that demanded attention. He was a professional who sought the truth and stood up for what was right. Eddie was flexible and quick to make decisions but he could change his opinions in response to new information. He did not back down once he came to understand the facts.

The water controversy was a complex political issue with many players:

- Environmental Protection Agency (EPA)

- Federal Department of Health, Education and Welfare (HEW)

- Oregon Board of Health

- Benton County Commissioners

- City of Albany

- City of Adair Village

- North Albany Service District Advisory Board

- Residents of other North Albany water districts

- Outlying customers on Adair water

- Pacific Power and Light Company (PP&L)

- The media

After attending many meetings, we began to understand what those facts were and piece together the bigger picture:

1) The state was threatening to force North Albany to annex to Albany because of the health hazard from contaminated wells.

2) Benton County was responsible to clear up the health hazard or the state would step in with forced annexation. The county was thinking of a possible contract with PP&L, but PP&L was not interested because of the prohibitive cost.

3) Albany City Council saw nothing wrong with continuing their delayed annexation procedures, while Eddie Hoops was refusing to allow that to continue.

4) Adair Village was faced with possible escalating water costs or loss of connection to the water and sewer plants.

We were already on the water and sewer lines and North Albany was not. We were the ones being threatened with shut-off, not them, and that was serious to us. In the Adair City Council meeting we drew up a resolution to apply for the plants from HEW ourselves.

A water agency can't just shut off water to its users, but Albany continued to give us shut off notices every two weeks. That was not a good way to live. We were the city council now and our citizens were depending on us.

We invited Albany's Mayor Leonard Roche for lunch along with three other Albany City Council members and three council members from Adair Village. Jim Ableman described our situation as, "Kind of between a rock and a hard place." We told Mayor Roche that we needed that water plant but couldn't afford it. He was polite to us and very communicative. We learned from him that Albany was also in the same boat financially as we were. They needed to extend water to North Albany, but could not afford to do an immediate annexation, which involves sewers, roads, police, fire protection, maintenance, repairs, and such. If the state forced annexation, then the city's new responsibility for North Albany would bankrupt the city. There was some talk of North Albany taking over the water plant and we thought our water rates would sky rocket if that happened.

Mayor Roche assured us that our water and sewer services would be continued. To his thinking, Albany would eventually grow to the point of needing the Adair system and he believed the city would grow beyond what PP&L could provide them from the Santiam River in the future. He hoped things could somehow work out for Albany to keep the plants and also keep their city delayed annexation requirements, which would provide for slow and stable growth. He was a future thinker and his goal was to protect Albany, just as ours was to protect Adair Village. We told the mayor that we would like to keep a friendly relationship with Albany. We felt the best scenario was for Albany to keep the plants because we believed that if North Albany controlled the water plant, they would raise our water rates to help cover their water system development expenses.

The Camp Adair sewer plant was also given to Albany as part of their quitclaim deed, but its small size and location, adjacent to Adair Village, made it unusable to North Albany. The controversy did not include the sewer plant. It was inconsequential.

Little did we realize what was in store for us and what events would transpire in the coming months. Councilwoman Michele Ryker planted a seed when she suggested that if there were any way that Adair Village could operate the plants, she preferred that Albany not have them. Albany officials told us they would consider operating the plants on a contractual basis at a fair wholesale rate. We needed to figure out what that might mean and what to do next. We were also concerned about higher water rates in the future. Albany had recently raised our rates.

We knew at that time we didn't really have adequate funds to own and operate the plants. However, Chuck Phillips felt we should not eliminate the possibility that Adair Village could run the water plant in conjunction with North Albany.

Delores Pollard

The Adair water plant seen from Highway 20 headed east.

Chapter 7: Tides of Controversy

February 8, 1978, at their regular Wednesday night meeting, Albany quietly announced that they just might keep the plants! They decided not to revert them, after all. What followed this announcement was a big if. *If* the government would simply allow Albany to continue to dictate its own terms for selling water, then the plants would stay in operation and everything would be fine. We were guaranteed two more weeks of water service. After that, they might cease operation and let it revert back to HEW.

This was no consolation at all. We decided right then to inform HEW that we wanted the plants for ourselves. We asked our lawyer to inform the Albany City Council that we would submit our intention to apply for the plants the minute they officially gave them up. Albany hadn't expected us to ask for them. Who were we? A new little city of no importance. They thought we shouldn't be worried about it. They believed we should be satisfied with their wholesale rate proposal. They felt we should trust them when they told us nothing would change in the way they were serving water to Adair Village. But we didn't like the threats to our water service. We didn't like the two-week notices. We were beginning to understand why the protestors in North Albany felt like pawns in a game that Albany officials were playing against the federal government in order to get their annexation policy accepted. We didn't know exactly how much it would cost for us to run the plants, but we decided that if we had to be financially responsible for them, then we might as well own them.

Charline

I remember when we applied for the Adair water and sewer plants. If Albany gave them up and someone else was to get them, we wanted it to be us. I felt that if we owned them we would be in charge of our own destiny. At least we wouldn't be hung out to dry if some other city decided to shut off our water.

If we operated the water plant together with North Albany, we would need the support of Benton County to get organized and financial help from federal funding to get the bonds we needed to pay for it.

The Benton County Commissioners got wind of our application for the plants. They met with HEW to talk about becoming the owner of the plants if Albany lost them. We never knew what was said in any of the conversations between the commissioners and Eddie, but Commissioner Barbara Ross officially stated that she did not support Adair Village owning the plants; she preferred that Albany keep running them.

One newspaper reporter assured us that we had nothing to worry about because HEW would not allow any of us to go without water. He joked that, "Even if Eddie Hoops has to carry the water in person, Adair Village will have water." This attitude in general was passed on to the public from Eddie Hoops' superior. The survival of Adair Village was a primary motivation for Hoops' allegiance to us. Eddie met with about 200 North Albany people and told them that his primary concern was the Adair Village residents who were already connected to the Adair water system. Besides, Eddie liked us. We were developing a good relationship with him. We were new, enthusiastic and positive and we were really a very tight and well-organized group. His support inspired confidence in us to step up and take care of our new city and ourselves.

Gazette Times

Eddie talking to Michele Ryker at a meeting in Albany.

This battle between HEW and Albany went on and on. Contrary to the hopes Albany held, Eddie Hoops stood firm on his refusal to yield to their annexation demands. Eddie Hoops was responsible for the Adair water plant and systems. Eddie had to make a hard decision about what to do, since Albany refused to comply with the regulations of their deed. Eddie refused to change the deed. He said the government would accept the reversion of the plants if that became necessary. He would probably give them to Benton County if it did not cause a financial burden on them, but only until North Albany, or Adair Village, was ready to take them over.

The Benton County Commission

Chairman Larry Callahan 1975-79

Benton County has three commissioners, elected countywide for a four year term. There is a rotating chairman, but all three share equal power. Board action requires at least two of the commissioners to be in agreement.

Commissioner Barbara Ross 1977-85

The national Advisory Commission on Intergovernmental Relations recognized county government in Oregon in 1978 as having the highest degree of local discretionary authority of any state in the nation. As legislative and executive officials, they both enact laws and administer them.

Commissioner Dale Schrock 1974-90

Each commissioner oversees one or more of the county departments. The board collects taxes for state and local governments; borrows and appropriates money; fixes the salaries of county employees; supervises elections; builds and maintains highways and bridges; and administers national, state and county welfare programs, among other things.

Photos: Benton County Board of Commissioners' Archives

On February 9, 1978 Albany made a new proposition to offer water to both Adair Village and North Albany on a wholesale rate basis and to drop the annexation requirements for serving water to North Albany. We followed up with a meeting to ask the city officials exactly what this would mean for us. We learned some of the problems this would cause for Adair Village. With this new proposal we would:

1) Share the cost of the equipment and the maintenance of the North Albany water lines,

2) Share the cost of Albany's administrative overhead for billing customers.

This would not be good for us. It was not something we were willing to do. We returned to Eddie and asked that HEW revert the plant from Albany and give it to Adair Village.

On February 10, Benton County Commissioners met with Eddie Hoops and agreed that the county could operate the plants until either North Albany or Adair Village could take them over. Benton County and Albany were working on land-use planning goals, water district boundaries and urban growth boundaries with some consideration of negotiation with PP&L as an alternative to the Adair plant hook-up. There was some question about the new land-use laws relating to the outlying farms and houses that were not within the taxable district of Albany.

The State Board of Health required Benton County to solve the health hazard problems. There was pressure on the county from real estate developers who were impatient to get back to construction work on the sites where the building moratorium had halted their progress. The State Board of Health would not lift the halt on permits until after the water problem for North Albany was resolved.

There was a lot on the Commissioners' plates. They had to propose plans to clean up the area's water, to formulate the water-service district, to outline a timetable for all this to be done, and to determine where the district would get its water, as well as detail any problems that might come up. By showing progress toward these goals, a hearing set for March 15 to force annexation of North Albany could be averted to a later date. Hopefully, that would give everyone more time to solve the problems.

We learned from Albany officials that the plants had been running on a deficit for years, and water prices would have to go up as much as 300 percent or maybe as much as 500 percent in order to meet the service needs of North Albany. Adair residents might soon be paying an increase from the current $5 to $16, for a base amount of 7,500 gallons. If a contingency fund for replacement of equipment was implemented, the rate could go as high as $27, with sewer also increasing from $7 to $24 or higher a month.

We met with Phillip Griffin, Chairman of the North Albany Water Service District Advisory Board, to talk about a partnership. We discussed the possibility of operating the water plant together. But North Albany wanted time to conduct surveys about what annexation to Albany might look like and how the residents felt about getting their water from Adair Village. They raised questions about the legality of such a coalition and the legality of Albany's forced delayed annexation agreements. They asked HEW headquarters for an immediate audit of Albany's records on the cost of running the plant. These were complex issues. The cost of maintaining and repairing the plant would become a big concern in the final decisions made later on.

At first, Eddie Hoops was not too hot on the idea of Adair Village receiving the plants because, as the government official, it was his job to try to resolve things with the original deed holder in these situations. It looked as if Albany was relenting and would keep the plants. But Eddie said that if he believed Adair Village could financially handle it, he would give serious consideration to us.

To have a stable supply of water for Adair Village was our first concern, but then to have water to sell to make money to operate the plants, well, that seemed like a very good plan. I'm sure everyone involved was thinking the same thing. There was a lot of future growth forecast for the North Albany area. Not only that, but the water rights were worth millions of dollars. We didn't know that at the time. That was never the big issue for us. That was on the periphery. It was never our focus.

✦

Chapter 8: The Big Decision

I must have been a boring person in those days because all I talked about was water, water, and water. It had engulfed my attention, so to speak.

Eddie Hoops gave Albany three days to abandon all annexation requirements, or he would take back the plants *for good* by the close of the business day on May 1. Take back the plants for good!

When the Albany City Council met on April 26, there was no quorum present to vote on Eddie's ultimatum. They asked him to extend the deadline for their response that Albany give up ALL of their annexation demands or else HEW would revert the plants and convey them to someone else. But the big question was: To whom?

Eddie was the kind of person who understood his job well and took his responsibilities very seriously. He drew from 17 years of experience and cared about the people he worked with. He joked that he would probably change his mind three times on his drive home to

Seattle. "Don't quote me, but I'll probably go home and 'fall on my sword' over the decision."

An exhausted Eddie leaves for Seattle.

At this point Benton County and Adair Village were competing, but we were Eddie's first choice because we were already on the water and sewer lines. North Albany had acquired the legal authority to begin to make contracts and agreements on water issues and was ready to discuss taking on the plants, but Commissioner Callahan had told Eddie the county was not interested in owning them. The press had strengthened the idea that the county was out of the picture, but still we were nervous about where the commissioners stood. We were ready to take the plants but Eddie seemed to lean toward Benton County because of its stronger financial status, its experience, and compared to little Adair Village, its resource network. But was the county still interested? We didn't know and we needed to find out. We were anxious about Eddie's recent ultimatum. He was going to decide who would get the plants. We had been given them, well *almost* had them, then Albany decided to keep them, but now perhaps, again, Albany might lose them! What a circus! What were the county commissioners thinking?

We knew that of the three county commissioners, Larry Callahan favored dropping the idea of ownership by the county and allowing Adair Village to acquire the plants. Commissioners Barbara Ross and Dale Schrock held fast that Benton County wanted them, and they were doing everything possible to persuade Eddie to give the plants to the county. You see, it wasn't just the plants, their systems and the reservoirs and transmission lines, but it also was the extremely valuable water rights. It's a huge water right, acquired by the military in the early 1940's. The older a water right is, the more valuable it is. The commissioners were well aware of this, as was the Albany Mayor. We were the only ones then who did not realize the value. We just knew the plants were probably going to be taken away from Albany and we wanted them.

On the Sunday before the big May 1 deadline, an Adair Village councilmember, my old friend Lorraine Ruff and I were sitting around my house talking it over.

I wondered, "How can we find out where Benton County stands *this* week?"

One of us, I don't remember who, said, "Let's go talk to Larry Callahan."

"But it's Sunday!" I said.

Lorraine said: "Since it is Sunday, he'll probably be at home."

We looked up the home address of the Chairman of the Board of County Commissioners, Mr. Callahan, and found out where he lived. Not really so far from us. We decided to pay him a visit. It was a spur of the moment decision. It wouldn't hurt anything to visit him and find out where Benton County stood, would it? Perhaps he could tell us something that we needed to know. We drove to his house and showed up unexpectedly. We knocked on his door. We were nervous but when he saw who we were, he graciously invited us in.

We asked Larry for some clarity, saying, "We understand that you told Eddie Hoops that Benton County *does* want the plants now?" He replied that, personally, he didn't think it was a good idea, but the county had been thinking of applying for them.

"Oh, you are?" We went on, "But didn't you tell Mr. Hoops at one time that you did not want them?"

"Yes, we did say that." He agreed.

"But you have changed your mind?" we asked.

He thought so, kind of. He told us he didn't think it was a great idea to have the county run the plants, but because of the water rights, he could see the wisdom in it. The fact that Larry mentioned the water rights just went completely over our heads. We had only a vague idea what he meant by that so we skirted the issue and moved right on ahead with our questions.

We knew the big decision was coming up, so we took a gamble and asked him outright, "Well, if you are not really that interested in taking them, why don't you let Eddie Hoops know that?"

It was intense. I think we were all holding our breaths. We expected him to say that he could not do that without talking to his other two commissioners. We expected to be bid goodbye right then and there. But to our surprise he said, Ok.

We couldn't believe it. We wiggled another inch forward. I asked, "Is that a promise? Can we count on you that you will let him know?"

We expected that he would say something like he is not the only one to make such decisions, or that he would have to talk with the other commissioners in their regular Wednesday meeting, or something similar. But he didn't say any of that. He just said yes again.

So Lorraine stepped up and asked. "When? If that is the case, how about now?"

I was really sweating and nervous. The room seemed to be deadly quiet; we were so focused on what was transpiring.

"It's Sunday," Larry said, "He is not there."

Lorraine piped up with, "He will probably be at home then. You wouldn't have to go through his office."

"I don't have his number," he said,

"I do," she said,

He could have said, "Hey, wait a minute. I am not going to do this." He could have said that at any point after he had opened the door. But he responded with, "Oh, Okay!" as if that idea had never occurred to him.

And Lorraine- always a "woman of the moment," asked, "Would you like me to dial it for you?"

I thought that would be the end of it. I expected him to refuse, but miraculously he said, "No, I think I can dial that myself." We were standing right there, and he called Eddie Hoops!

We listened attentively, probably all leaning forward, big eyed, mouths hanging open. I remember it vividly. We watched and I could tell when Eddie Hoops came to the phone. Larry identified himself and then said he was calling to inform Eddie that Benton County was not interested in having the Adair water plant.

It was exactly that! We heard it with our own ears. It was a short conversation but oh, so sweet to us. We could hardly contain ourselves. We thanked him and quickly left. Out in the car we nearly went into shock. What had happened in there? Did he really call Eddie? We were amazed and delighted and confused. Why did he do that? He was not tentative at all. He must really have not wanted the plants.

We didn't talk much on the way home. In fact, we never talked about it again. Not between ourselves and not to anyone. It seemed like a miracle had occurred and I was just overwhelmed, and I think Lorraine and the councilmember were, too. We didn't quite know what to make of it. Like a gift horse, we didn't want to examine it too closely. We went to our separate homes feeling like something amazing had just happened.

Eddie called me the next morning. It was Monday, May 1, the day of the ultimatum. He said to me, "You'll never believe what those county commissioners have done now! They changed their minds again."

I paused for a heartbeat then asked, "Oh, how do you know that?" I just played dumb.

He said. "Well, I got a call yesterday afternoon, at my house, from Larry Callahan and you know he is the chairman of the Benton County Commissioners?"

I said, "Yes, I know that."

He continued, "Well, I can tell you, I am tired of fooling around with them. First they want the plants and then they don't, then they do and then they don't. I am going to give the plants to Adair Village."

He knew we had been steady all the way through the process and had wanted them from the beginning. It appeared to Eddie that the Benton County Commissioners had "waffled" on their commitments to run the plants temporarily. Eddie used that word to the press when describing how he felt about it. The commissioners denied having waffled but Commissioner Callahan admitted that he had not been on the same page with the other two about the county taking over the responsibility of the water plant.

Commissioner Dale Schrock had been at many of the water districts' meetings and had often stated that they had a majority of the commissioners behind the county's decision to run the plant for North Albany. But anytime Eddie sought conformation he called the county's main office in Corvallis and got the Board Chairman, Larry Callahan, who was not behind the idea. Chairman Callahan had concerns about the financial aspects for Benton County so the answers Eddie had received from the three commissioners over the last three months were inconsistent.

After Eddie hung up with me, he immediately called the newspapers for a press conference. He was fed up with both Albany and Benton County. Perhaps he, too, could be said to be acting on the spur of the moment, because that very day, Monday, May 1, he flew down from Seattle and filed the reversion papers in the Benton County Courthouse, and then drove out to Adair Village to give us the temporary operating permits!

At an emergency city council meeting that evening, the City of Adair Village voted unanimously to accept the plants. Eddie explained the deed and the requirements we would have to meet, and went back home to Seattle.

And that is how the little City of Adair Village got its sewer and water plants, the reservoirs, all of the systems and the water rights.

And that was the end of that.

Delores: Would Eddie have given the plants to Benton County if Larry Callahan had not called him on Sunday and said they didn't want them?

Charline: Yes, probably. We will never know for sure what else might have happened. But I think he felt that Benton County was in a better position to operate the systems than we were. It was implied that we were too young, too inexperienced, and too poor. But we had already applied for the plants early on and never vacillated.

Delores: That call to Eddie appears to be what swung it in your direction. You didn't tell your city council about that Sunday visit?

Charline: No! Our lips were sealed. We didn't even make that agreement between us! We just all kept our mouths shut. I don't know why. None of that was ever known.

Wanda: You never even told *me*!

Charline: Wanda, I know. I never even told my own husband. At this point I am almost embarrassed about it, and I guess that you think I should be, especially because we were best friends, working together every day. But I didn't tell anyone! We three were grateful for the way it had happened. We didn't know what to say about it.

Delores: Did Eddie know?

Charline: I never told him. He never mentioned it

Wanda: Well, the truth is the truth.

Delores: Some secrets are worth keeping. Others are too good to keep forever.

Chapter 9: Up and Running

The Adair water plant belonged to Adair Village! We were ecstatic. Our worries of having our water shut off were over. We celebrated with high hopes and set about with our innate fervor to meet the requirements of our federal deed. Eddie Hoops fooled Albany. He *did* revert the plants and he *did* have a place to put them and that was with Adair Village! The days and nights spent writing letters and proposals to justify why Adair Village should have them paid off. In the meantime, of course, Albany said, "Oh, wait a minute. Let's give some more consideration to this." But Eddie answered, "Too late."

Not everyone was happy about Eddie's decision. Commissioner Barbara Ross immediately announced the county would apply for ownership of the plants because the residents of North Albany would become the primary users. But it was pretty much assumed Adair Village was going to serve water to North Albany. It said so in our deed, after all.

We had a lot to learn and fast! Bill Carr was involved in everything about the undertaking, and it was a tremendous undertaking. We had a short list of things we had to do. One of the first was to hire a plant operator. Waiting in the wings was Sam Goff, who had been trained at Linn-Benton Community College and had experience working on municipal utilities.

Our public works director, lawyer, accountant, another councilmember and I met with the Albany staff on May 5, just four days after Eddie had publically given us the plants. Albany City Manager Hugh Hull said he was glad it was over. "It's been a long, hard squabble," he said. He was happy the "albatross" was no longer his problem. It was highly unlikely that Albany would dispute the action in court. Residents inside the city limits had pressured the Albany council to stop worrying about people outside the city limits.

Albany presented us with a list of equipment that would stay with the plants. Our lawyer went through a line item inventory to see what equipment had been purchased with water revenue money and should remain with the plant. A pick-up truck, a pump, a motor, a chlorinator, a scales and a desk were returned to Albany. Unfortunately, the chlorinator they left with us broke down in July. We had to spend $400 to fix it.

It was agreed that Albany would receive the prorated funds up until May 15, and Adair Village would receive the revenue from that point forward. We were pleased that Albany agreed to provide maps and charts at no cost to us, which showed the locations of some of the water and sewer lines.

Gazette Times

Sam Goff, our first water plant employee, May 15, 1978.

We were determined to do our first meter reading on May 26 and would bill at Albany's regular billing time. Lou suggested that there be no rate hike until we had operated the plants for a period of time. Albany had used a Salem company to do their billing by computer, and Lou offered to look into the cost of continuing that system, but we had no computer then and no funds to buy one. Wanda ended up doing our billing, storing the file cabinets in her house, using her kitchen table as her office desk, and computing bills with a hand calculator.

The water plant permit that had been held by Albany was granted to Adair Village from the Corps of Engineers. I don't remember if we had to pay for that. We also had to apply for an intake permit; a chlorine storage permit and a discharge permit for the sewer from the Department of Environmental Quality (DEQ). These permits are required for any city that has water and wastewater treatment plants and were some of the first things we needed.

Liability insurance coverage had to be established before Sam could begin work on May 15. Insurance was mandatory and cost the city $3,000 per year.

The buildings had to be appraised for insurance coverage. For the property and related personal property insurance, the company needed to know how many people would be hired, the number of gallons of water sold, and the number of miles of sewer lines involved! Bill Carr gathered this information from Albany in less than a week. The insurance policy for liability, fire, and vandalism coverage cost us $1,200 a year.

Our financial responsibilities were adding up fast. We were trying to get a bank loan for the immediate costs of the take-over, but it was slow in coming. For immediate expenses we passed a resolution authorizing an intra-fund loan from our street fund for up to $5,000. Our city's yearly revenue was a pitiful $21,000.

We scrambled under a probation period of 120 days in which to prove we could handle the plants, or we could lose them. We had to be ready to sell water to North Albany, because that was a requirement in our federal deed just as it had been for Albany. We knew we would need funds to operate so we began the further investigation of the possibility of a $175,000 Farmers Home Administration loan. In our enthusiasm, we gave North Albany a deadline of May 19 to decide if they wanted to buy water from us. But the county wanted time to study things. Commissioner Ross asked for an extension of 6 weeks. This seemed like a dreadful waste of time to us.

The point was that we needed to complete an engineering study that would give us the figures for an estimated rate structure.

Wanda

As owners of the water plant, we suddenly had to create a billing system. Sam Goff, our water plant operator, had to drive around and read all the meters, and I am not sure he ever read meters before. We had our meter book, which we made ourselves. Sam gave the readings to me to record. For example, the work went something like this: Charline Carr...x number of gallons used. And then everyone else's use was recorded and then totaled up. I had to crosscheck everything to make sure the number of gallons that came out of the water plant was in some proportion to loss and use, and to make sure that I hadn't overcharged or forgotten anyone.

The county paid for the engineering study. They also approached Pacific Power and Light (PP&L) and asked them to provide an estimate to supply water to North Albany. So far, PP&L had been reluctant to get involved because of the cost. PP&L would have to add a water pipe in addition to the sewer pipe previously installed over the Willamette River and also revamp their intake facilities on the Santiam River. They were still not interested in making any estimates. It was late May, and we had until August 28 to prove we could handle the plants before we received the official deed.

We contacted the North Albany Service District Advisory Board to begin negotiations for the expected hook-up, but they were not a unified group. Opinions differed. We learned that many of the local water districts wanted to investigate the possibility of acquiring water from PP&L!

The Parker-Oak Grove water district was not happy with Eddie. They were in the water service business and had expected the water plant to revert to them through Benton County. Phil Griffin, chairman of the board for the new North Albany Special Service District, was so upset with Eddie's quick decision that he resigned. He felt Eddie had not listened to them nor considered all the options and was dismayed at what he termed Hoops' "cart-before-the–horse" decision. North Albany had become eligible to receive the plants just 12 days before Eddie gave them to us. Some feathers were ruffled that would never be unruffled, but the deed was done. These disgruntled people renewed interest in PP&L. Parker-Oak Grove Water District Chairman Jack Parker was concerned that the upcoming $2.5 million bond election to finance the water solution proposed that water service come only from Adair Village. Jack requested an immediate estimate from PP&L to compare the cost of services. Parker-Oak Grove had sent prior petitions asking the County Commissioners to research PP&L as an alternative to Adair Village.

Commissioner Barbara Ross again told Eddie Hoops the county would submit an application for ownership of the plants, even though he had signed them over to Adair Village. She pledged to support Adair Village but wanted to be able to take over if the "fledgling city" of Adair Village failed. The County Commissioners publicly backed us, but let it be known that they held grave doubts about our ability to handle the responsibility. Eddie apparently had no such doubts.

He told the commissioners he would consider their application, but that since most of the water lines were within the incorporated city limits of Adair Village, we had the proprietary rights. He said he had no reason to change his decision. The plants were back home. Eddie meant what he said, as we had all seen. He thought he was finished with making decisions about the Adair water plant controversy.

Delores Pollard

View of the Adair water plant from the east side.

On May 27, the Dumbeck water district approached us and requested that its district and the Palestine water district receive water services from us. Those districts were on wells and they needed a clean source of water. The lines that served the 208 homes were in good condition. We drew up a contract with Dumbeck, which brought 55 residences into our system. Palestine did not come on board with us.

Delores

Why did Dumbeck sign up with you?

Charline

Through all these meetings, so many meetings with Albany, with all the water districts, Wanda and I became close friends with a woman named Gail Olson. She was the secretary and her dad, Virgil Williams, was the chairman of the Dumbeck water district. There was an affinity between us and we got to know them very well and. Virgil believed in Adair. His whole board believed we would succeed. He did not believe the plants would be reverted from us, like they had been from Albany.

The Hurleywood water district requested water services because contaminated water had gotten in their lines through a damaged pump. A legal snag arose in our water district agreement with the county in which the sale of water to customers outside our urban growth boundary was prohibited. The paperwork on this wasn't yet finalized so we were able to strike that provision from the agreement. Hurleywood received water from us for a short time.

We sold water to all of the residences and buildings in Adair Village, the Trade School and the Fish and Wildlife Department. Gary and Lola Brumbaugh lived up Rondo Drive behind the water plant. When we signed the agreement to sell water to them in 1978, the hookup fee was $306. Richard and Carol Gilsdorf lived along Independence Highway toward Voss Hill. In the old days you could make some friendly deals without so much legal hassle. Life was much simpler. We made an easement agreement with them that gave them free water if they would maintain our road for us. Sometimes people would go up there, leave trash and make a big mess. We wanted our road watched over to keep that from happening.

Repair of the roof at Voss Hill Reservoir was part of the original deed that we inherited from Albany, but they had not completed the engineering studies for this obligation. Eddie gave us one year to get this done. We interviewed engineering firms and hired Dick Nored of HGE Inc. as our city engineer to repair the reservoir roof. This firm stayed with us for years.

Delores Pollard

Cook's barn from Ryals Lane in summer 2012. Voss Hill reservoir
is behind the trees to the left at the top of the hill.

We knew it was critical to get accurate figures on
the cost of providing water to North Albany.
Information had to be gathered about their water needs,
which included the compatibility of their different water
district systems and the cost of upgrading the Adair
plant in order to provide the necessary quantity of water.

The county engineer, Jim Blair, contracted HGE
Inc., the engineer for Adair Village, to do the study on
the feasibility for getting water to North Albany by
Adair Village as well as by PP&L. Benton County did
not receive an estimate from PP&L, however. They
were still not interested. This project estimate was
finished by July. The rates to North Albany were
estimated at a base rate of $17.05 per household per

month for wholesale water from Adair Village. This covered the cost of payback for North Albany's $2.5 million loan, the cost of consolidation of the water districts, the water line hook-ups and the wholesale price of water from the Adair water plant for 2000 people. James Blair supported the estimates at the time.

Eddie called me in June and said that he had decided to make our temporary deed permanent. Our 120-day probation period had only run for 49 days. He said he wanted to do it as of June 20. This would be accomplished with a quitclaim deed and would include a reverser deed in escrow, which would allow HEW to revert the plants if Adair Village could not successfully operate them. He requested that I come to Seattle, get the deed and then deliver the documents to the Benton County records department in Corvallis.

I remember we had to scrape together money for the trip. The city council made a resolution to allot $100 for my plane ticket. Eddie met me at the airport and we went straight to his office. We went over the paperwork, then out to lunch.

James Blair was 30 years old when he was named the first full-time Benton County engineer and public works director in 1973.

He held a bachelor's of science degree in civil engineering from OSU, and an associate degree in highway technology from the Oregon Technical Institute of Klamath Falls. He lived in Albany and had been employed by the Linn County Engineer's Office since 1970. He had worked as a consultant civil engineer and a land surveyor.

Eddie said to me, "You know, Charline, these water rights are worth a LOT of money." I didn't even think to ask him how much money. At that time, we didn't really pay much attention to the value of water rights. We were more concerned about where the water was going to go; first to Adair Village residents and then to other entities. Nobody talked much about the water rights during the controversy, and only later we learned they were worth millions! Albany's Mayor Roche mentioned them in early newspaper stories, but water rights were not a topic of discussion at any of the hundreds of meetings we had attended through the winter and spring. I wasn't even a bit curious about why

Eddie wanted to finalize the deed early. Lorraine had heard rumors that Eddie was receiving pressure from his supervisors at GSA to wrap up the water controversy. Whatever the reason, we were happy about it. We finally had the DEED to the Adair water plant!

Wanda	I remember Lorraine Ruff and I made the dress you wore to meet Eddie to get the deed to the water plant!
Charline	I remember it was at my house and she brought her sewing machine over. You two worked on that all night for me. You sewed. I tried on. You sewed more. I tried on. I didn't have any really dressy dress to wear that was appropriate. In those days you wore nylons and high heels to dress up. Anyway, so I looked good.
Judi	What was the dress like?

Charline

It was peach and brown. It was a soft fabric - a skirt, a sleeveless top and a jacket. And they sewed it *all in one night!*

Wanda

Oh, my gosh! Yes! That is a heap of sewing!

Charline

I just remember that I really felt top-notch. Here I go on the plane!

⊛

Chapter 10: Summer of Hope

We received the water plant together with the wastewater treatment plant, which was minor in comparison, but both were on the quitclaim deed. A month later the Oregon Department of Environmental Quality (DEQ) sent us a notice that indicated we were unknowingly violating a section of our wastewater discharge permit. The DEQ requested that we install additional lines to the south and east of the wastewater treatment plant. We also needed to make a lagoon that would hold three days of discharge should there be a mechanical breakdown! We wondered why Albany had not addressed these problems. The cost of these improvements was about $118,000. We also required a flow meter, which cost $6,000 more. We immediately began to apply for grants.

When the engineer began the work to cut down all the trees along the ditch, someone from Fish and Wildlife saw that, and called her supervisors. They told us we would have to replace the trees, because it was in a protected wetland area! Senate Bill 100 identified land uses and resources by new state guidelines. Wetlands!

Delores Pollard

Part of the Adair sewer treatment plant east of Adair Park.

Judi: I have been working with the file on the wastewater plant about putting in the main line under the railroad.

Delores: Did they have to remove the railroad track to put the pipeline in?

Judi: No, they went under it, but it was about 18 feet under. They had to drill way down to put the pipe in. The inspectors had to be there on the spot when it was done and the work could not interfere with any train schedules. It was stipulated exactly when it could be done. And we had to pay a lot of money in order to do that project.

Wanda: We had to replant everything that they had cut out. They had also enlarged the pond for the sewer plant. Someone from Tom's Gardens came over and looked at the plants that were left, told us what they were, and got them for us. It wasn't so bad planting all the trees; it was all those little wetland plants that were hard, the ones around the edges of the pond. Some of them were plants that actually lived in the water.

By July we were in hot water, so to speak. Our accountant advised us to add a 25% surcharge to all water and sewer bills starting in August. This rate increase would enable us to create an emergency reserve fund, a requirement of our deed. Our engineering study was finished and it indicated that we would run an annual deficit of $1,800. If North Albany connected to us, we would be okay, but if not, we would be forced to raise our water rates again in the near future. So much for lowering costs as the owners of the plants!

At the beginning of August, North Albany still had not made a commitment to us for water service. Benton County wanted Adair Village to contribute $1.4 million as our share of the cost to get water from the Adair plant to North Albany. We believed we could get a bond for that amount. North Albany was applying for a bond of $2.5 million to fund the project. PP&L was still refusing to become involved.

Bill and I went to Seattle to a conference on wastewater plants. Bill really needed to learn about this. It was a two-day seminar. We went up there, stayed in a hotel room and to us it was awe-inspiring. Here we were in the big city,

Charline

learning about wastewater treatment, which most people would find rather boring. But we didn't! We went through the seminar but as an aside, we had left at home two darling toy poodles. They had never slept away from us. They slept with us, on our bed. So, we had a couple of Wanda's boys stay at our house so the puppies could sleep with them. I called a few times to make sure they were all right. But it just goes to show how, well, unsophisticated we were then.

Richard Nored of HGE Inc. had formulated a proposed project cost of $3.3 to $3.5 million. The proposal also warned there would be an expense to *rebuild the entire Adair water system sometime in the future!* This expense was not covered in the $1.4 million bond that would be necessary to expand the Adair water plant. Little did we know what power lay coiled within that simple phrase "to rebuild the entire system."

Benton County was seeking $1.6 million for the project. A county plan proposed water to North Albany for as low as a million dollars, which sounded appealing to many. But this scaled-down plan left the old water pipes on the hills in North Albany, which was criticized by other engineers as a potential disaster. The existing systems in the 13 water districts operated at different water pressures and could not be connected together easily. Jim Blair suggested that the best solution would be for Adair Village to keep the water plant and to serve North Albany with water at a wholesale rate.

It was estimated that North Albany would need four million gallons of water per day, Adair Village and its surrounding customers used about 600,000 gallons per day. The water plant currently produced 1.3 to 1.9 million gallons per day. For about $400,000 new filters and the repair of other equipment would raise that volume to five million gallons per day. That would be sufficient for the needs of North Albany and Adair Village. For an additional $500,000 (not that much when considering the estimated $3 - $3.5 million total cost of the whole project), the water plant could easily produce 10 million gallons per day. We had been told that was the amount produced during the 1940's when the plant was new and Camp Adair was the second largest population center in Oregon.

On September 1, 1978 an offer from PP&L was finally submitted to North Albany. It was proposed to cost $100,000 more a year than the Adair Village option for connecting the 13 water districts. This offer was rejected unless PP&L reduced this estimated cost. In addition, the projected financing needs for the Adair hook-up would be $399,450 but with PP&L it would be a minimum of $496,910. Hooking up to Adair Village would save about $97,460 a year, at the least. This presentation of facts and figures showed that Adair would be the most economical and logical choice.

When PP&L renegotiated their figures, the county wanted them lowered even further but it didn't look like PP&L would do that. The paper quoted Blair saying, "It is plainly obvious, long range planning leans towards Adair as being the most economical."

Commissioner Barbara Ross requested a comparative study between PP&L and Adair Village in mid-September. In this study, Harold Leedom, of Regional Construction Inc., made it clear that the cost of hooking up water to North Albany from either Adair Village or PP&L would "likely be about the same," but he concluded that the annual cost for the system would rise faster with PP&L. The headline read "Engineer picks Adair over PP&L proposal." He did not recommend the PP&L choice because of the lack of local control over rates and policies regarding the water supplied by PP&L.

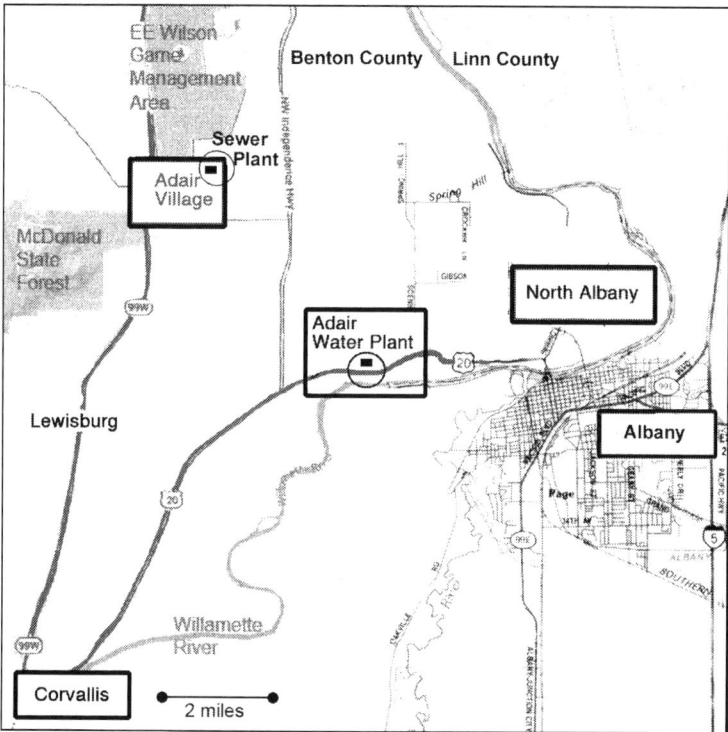

Delores Pollard

The location of the Adair water treatment plant near the Willamette River, between Adair Village and North Albany.

On September 27, North Albany agreed again to contract with Adair Village rather than PP&L for their water service. The headlines read " North Albany to Get Adair Water." The Commissioners had approved the recommendations and hoped to settle the contract by October 5. We would soon serve water to North Albany. We were happy and expected things to go well. Our water rates would not increase, North Albany would connect with us and use their revenues to help pay for the loan to upgrade the plant. We would be able to grow and prosper with the enticing new challenges of the near future. Everything looked rosy. At last!

Delores Pollard

Yet another view of the lovely Adair water plant.

Letter to the Editor in the *Gazette Times*:

Interested in outcome of water bond vote.

As a resident of Adair Village I am interested in the outcome of the bond election. And the decision to be made by the North Albany County Service District and /or the Benton County Commissioners to buy water from PP&L or Adair Village. My interest is a selfish one: my water bill will likely be lower (eventually) if North Albany buys water from Adair Village.

There is an interesting element, which has not been brought out in the news articles. PP&L is a corporation owned by stockholders. Its purpose as a business is to make a profit for the stockholders, and this they do by charging fees for needed utility services provided--- electricity and water.

The rates charged by PP&L are set by them (approved by the Public Utility Commissioner), with no required input from the patrons served. The rate charged will be subject to change and the users will have nothing to say about it.

The Adair water system, however, is a non-profit entity and cannot show a profit. A condition stipulated by HEW for Adair Village to continue ownership was that the users would play a part in determining the rates, through the formation of a representative water board, made up of residents of North Albany as well as Adair Village. I note with some interest the statements made

concerning the likely bias of the consultant hired by Benton County for the Water Service District, {ibid HGE Inc.} in view of the fact he also serves as city engineer for Adair Village. I find no fault with this comment. It is an understandable reaction.

Have all the facts been presented fairly, by the *Democrat Herald*, considering the "indirect" relationship it has with PP&L? The president of the paper is also the chairman of the executive committee of PP&L. Can we assume unbiased news coverage under these circumstances? I wonder.

William E. Tobiassen

Editor's Note: The answer to both questions posted in the concluding paragraph is yes.

Chapter 11: Power Struggles

We were looking forward to our opportunity to begin contracting water service to North Albany. We were in high spirits but did not know what issues would arise in our coming negotiations. Our involvement was intense as we moved toward a bright future for our little city. Recognizing the fact that we didn't have financial or political backgrounds, we were optimistic that things would work out for us. This belief bonded us together as a city council and we felt we would succeed. We soon were confronted with Benton County power politics, which boiled down to two controversial issues:

1) Rates and services: who would have the final say over general policies, capital improvements and operating budgets for the water plant, and

2) Disagreements over the service area boundaries.

This was referred to as "the great hook-ups debate." The commissioners sought veto power over anyone who wanted to buy water from Adair Village. We believed that anyone living outside the North Albany water districts should be able to buy water from us if they wanted to without consulting Benton County. If someone along the line wanted to hook up to us, they should have that choice and we should be allowed to legally sell water to them.

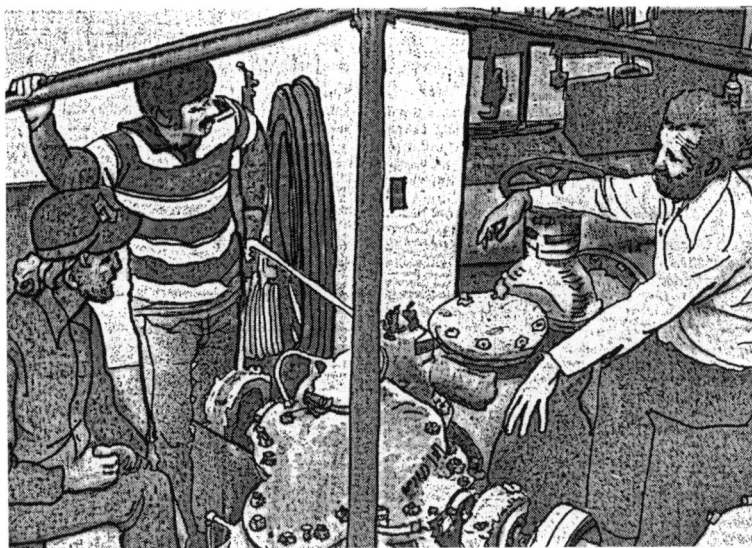

Gazette Times

September 15, 1978. LBCC's Paul Klopping (right) looks over a pump at the Adair water treatment plant with two graduates: Chief Operator Sam Goff (in the cap), and Ron Waggoner, (standing) his assistant.

Our federal deed stated that anyone who was willing to run water lines to us was to receive water at wholesale cost. There were 20 other contract negotiation points on both technical and administrative matters that were acceptable to all parties, but these two caused problems. Both issues involved money and control. The water plant brought with it millions of dollars worth of water rights. Who would control it?

Because the Benton County commissioners were the governing body responsible for making sure that North Albany received clean water, any contract we made with North Albany had to be approved by a majority of the commissioners. The contracts we successfully negotiated directly with North Albany were repeatedly rejected by Benton County. It took six weeks and nine renegotiated water service contracts before it become clear to Benton County that Eddie was not going to budge on his decision.

It was during these October negotiations that the words Eddie Hoops had spoken to me about the value of the water rights began to sink in. While I was waiting to board the plane back home from Seattle with the water plant deed and the water rights in my hand, I recall what he said to me and that moment remains one of my strongest and clearest memories. Eddie emphasized the value of the water rights and told me to honor what was now our responsibility. "Whatever happens," he warned, "Do not give up any control of the plant or the water rights." He implored me to refuse any terms that interfered with our city's management of them.

I believe the commissioners were trying to get Eddie to take the plants away from us. When considering this goal, their obstructionist tactics made sense. When the commissioners called on Eddie Hoops to come down to moderate the conflict, he refused to get involved. He publicly stated that he gave the plants to Adair Village because it seemed the most natural solution to the problem. He urged us all to work it out locally. But the county didn't seem to have faith in us, which was obvious by their many remarks. They seemed to stir up fears about what might happen if we were given the contracts.

One of the prevailing fears was that with new housing developments springing up in North Albany, homes would be exceedingly expensive because of the high taxes necessary in order to pay off loans for the Adair water plant. Another fear working against us was that we were too young, too inexperienced and too poor. We had five people on our city council and opponents questioned the fairness of these five people making decisions affecting the 2000 people in North Albany. Adair Village had less than 600 people with an assessed property tax value of $3.1 million. North Albany had an assessed value of $84 million for the entire area and $54 million for the area within the water service boundaries. We knew that realistically there would be some bumps and snags. We probably would need some financial assistance along the way, but I think we could have resolved the issues together, had they worked with us. We believed we could do it. We had a water plant. They needed water. What was the problem?

 **Charline** The "tiny" City of Adair Village was referred to in the media at one point as "the mouse that roared." This was a reference to a currently running British satirical comedy of that name, about a small European nation who declared war on the United States, attacked New York City, and inadvertently won the war. In our case the analogy applied to Adair Village going to war against big Benton County over control of the water plant.

Commissioner Ross was insisting that the people of North Albany get operational control of the Adair water plant. We were not going to let control of this water plant out of our hands. Eddie had warned us again and again about giving up control, and it was not going to happen here. Period.

We were responsible for the water plant for the next 30 years under the terms of our deed from HEW, and we could not give away our control to another governing body that might not abide by the rules of that deed. The commissioners wanted a *control board* with North Albany holding the majority voting power. We were fighting for an *advisory board* where Adair Village would maintain final say in all decisions relating to capital improvements and operating budgets.

To our chagrin, the October 13 newspaper headline read: "Control of Water Plant Pits Adair Against County." That was really exasperating. We thought things were working out in our favor! Things apparently *were not* working out. We felt it more appropriate to say that the big county was pitting itself against little us.

The people of the Parker-Oak Grove water district expressed disappointment that Chairman Larry Callahan had not applied for the plants from HEW for North Albany. Obviously these North Albany folks were still unhappy about the reversion to us. Eddie was criticized for not really wanting to help North Albany.

Adair Village was criticized for wanting power just to show off what "tiny Adair" could do. We didn't like this accusation. We didn't like the accusation of being on a power trip to prove to everyone how great we were. The characteristic word tiny stuck to our name like glue.

On October 17, we were frustrated when a newspaper interview with James Blair contained many misstatements about the water negotiations. The *Albany Democrat Herald* headline read: "Disagreements Block Water Deal for North Albany." James Blair publicly proposed three solutions to the North Albany water problem:

1) To "reason with the federal officials" to seriously reconsider negotiating with Benton County over ownership of the Adair water plant.

2) To negotiate a water contract with PP&L and leave Adair out of it completely.

3) To outright ask HEW to take the plants away from Adair Village and give them to North Albany.

We were stunned when we read of their strategies. Why were they *still* talking to HEW? We had been on the brink of a final contract with North Albany but it seemed the commissioners had moved us all back to square one. We realized that this probably had been going on between Eddie and Benton County since he gave us the plants. We have a copy of the October 17 newspaper article where, scribbled on the back in pencil, one of our councilmen wrote: "To Public Works Director: Childish! Don't give up before we have really begun to fight!"

All through the summer it had been generally assumed that Adair Village would serve water to North Albany. All the studies showed Adair Village was the best choice. Now, in the middle of October, Benton County wanted HEW to take the plant away from *us*? We owned the deed. Eddie had made sure of that. We read in the November 2, Salem *Statesman Journal*: "Commissioner Ross said she had personally made a commitment to the people of North Albany to make sure they had control of the system that they would be paying for." She suggested that another survey be conducted to poll the North Albany citizens to see just *how many* people really wanted Adair water. She reiterated that we had no experience running a large plant and she suggested PP&L was a safer option. Point after point was raised against us, stirring up distrust and fear. Commissioner Ross wondered how we had correctly determined the wholesale rate if the remodeling and enlarging costs were unknown. These rates had previously been produced by the public works director and by reputable engineering firms, yet the estimates were being questioned as if we had formulated them ourselves for our own ends.

Eddie told the press he was supportive of Adair Village holding onto the responsibility for the plants, but we must get on with the repair of the Voss Hill reservoir roof. Water for Adair Village came from that reservoir and Eddie was holding our feet to the fire to get this done. We had been given a year to do it and three months had already gone by. We requested an extension on the deadline but Eddie refused. I think he didn't want to give North Albany any grounds to call for a reversion. We didn't understand why we had to rush to do this, but we trusted Eddie and followed through with it.

We needed to set a date for the bond election for this repair and wanted to include the $1.4 million that we needed for the North Albany water service extension at the same time. However, Farmers Home Administration would not agree to finance this additional amount unless we had a solid contract from North Albany.

We sent a letter to the commissioners asking them to sign what we called our *final* contract with

North Albany. We set a deadline for their response because we needed to put the notice in the paper two weeks before the election date, which we had scheduled for November 21. The commissioners rejected the contract. Should we have been surprised?

Gazette Times

Railings along the settling tanks at the water plant.

Chapter 12: Last Ditch Effort

On November 7, 1978, North Albany approached us again with another contract offer. The newspaper presented it as North Albany trying to "bridge troubled waters." Their chairman said he believed things would work out after our talk and we all hoped for an end to the conflict with this new negotiation. I was very pleased. The breakthrough was a compromise that gave the joint water board greater authority on certain key items but retained the conditions that Adair Village needed to keep overall control. One member of the North Albany Water Service District favored the hard line approach to Adair Village, but the chairman was with us. He said, "If the agreement isn't signed, since we are the two parties in agreement, then we will know who is stopping this!"

The next day the North Albany Water District Service Board again made changes that blocked Adair's control. The changes were not acceptable to us. These board members were aligned with the county in their effort to get the plants. The newspaper reported: "Water negotiations nearing collapse."

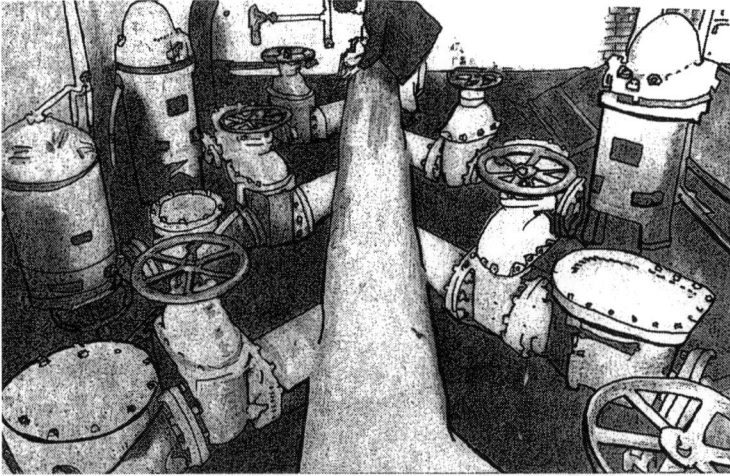

View of the pipes and valves inside the water plant circa 1972.

Eddie passed through Corvallis on November 13 and met with the Benton County Attorney Todd Brown. The commissioners were out of town and had asked Mr. Brown to discuss the contract and the terms of our ownership of the Adair treatment plant. Eddie agreed to see if he could help facilitate a settlement. The attorney wanted to know if the failure to form a joint water board was proof of failure to fulfill our deed. Eddie agreed to examine all the contracts to see if there was *any* legal reason for HEW to take the plants away from us. He was reluctantly trying to solve the problem that for him just would not go away. The county told Eddie they were ready to apply for the plants for North Albany. Apparently they never actually applied.

Following his examination of the contracts, Eddie told Todd Brown that another ownership transfer was unlikely and assured him that our contract proposal satisfied the requirements of our deed, as had the others as well. All nine contracts were consistent. There was no reason to revert the plants from us. He said we were "being very reasonable" and that we "could not give up control of what had been given to us."

In the *Democrat Herald* on November 11, Eddie repeated, "Adair Village owns the plant." He said, "They have to *offer* water to North Albany, but North Albany can't start demanding conditions, which would result in such absolute power that Adair Village no longer would have control. It is indeed a sad situation. I would have liked to see North Albany get water from Adair. It looked like a natural."

On November 21, our bond issue passed for the replacement of the Voss Hill reservoir roof. The action was duly noted in that we had not voted for a federal bond for the expansion of the plant. Some North Albany folks commented that we did not really want to help them. But Blair stood up for us and said we could still negotiate terms and get another federal bond for that.

When the commissioners returned to town, they learned the county attorney had again failed to get the plants reverted from us. Because the negotiations with Adair Village had broken down, because there was no reversion from HEW, and because no contract proposal gave North Albany the control she had promised them, Commissioner Barbara Ross finally gave up. It was time to move on. In the Benton County Board of Commissioners' Minutes Book (40, Page 17, November 22, 1978), Barbara Ross and Dale Schrock voted 2-1 to authorize James Blair to "go to PP&L and bring back a contract." Larry Callahan voted no.

Mr. Blair then turned 180 degrees from supporting us to supporting PP&L. He changed his estimates to cover costs for replacement of the entire Adair plant, under the assumption that it would wear out someday, and this showed that Adair water was not such a good idea after all. He explained that he had neglected to adjust the numbers to cover the cost of a capital fund, which he said was necessary in order to replace the entire plant. This didn't make sense to us. His new "reasonable and conservative projection," as he called it, showed Adair would cost over $1.2 million dollars more than PP&L.

By factoring in this unrealistic capital fund, of course PP&L suddenly appeared to be the most economical way to go! Commissioner Ross said she was satisfied to sign with PP&L because the cost would be fair, and the rates stable and predictable. The Leedom estimates done in September had said this was absolutely not true. But Ross justified her trust in PP&L by pointing out they had been in business for a long time, were professional, and knew what they were doing, implying that we did not. In fact, there were quotes from me in the newspaper very early on admitting that very thing. My naive statements were used against me. We were not being given the chance to prove ourselves.

We were shocked. But we would not give up easily. We wrote a letter of protest to the chairman of the board and had it printed in the *Gazette Times* on November 30. In this letter, we explained how the capital fund was *not at all* how James Blair portrayed it. I requested that his miscalculation be corrected immediately. Our need for a capitol fund actually was a mere $10,000 not the $1.2 million as he had claimed. It was really just a reserve fund for emergencies such as equipment failure. There was never a plan to raise enough money to replace the entire plant! I explained that Jim Blair was completely amiss to have calculated that sum onto our cost estimate. The replacement of the whole plant might be a consideration *sometime* in the future, as far away as 40 years. Replacing the entire plant had nothing at all to do with the current cost of establishing water service to North Albany. But PP&L was now committed to sell water to North Albany, leaving Adair Village completely out.

It doesn't make any difference what the truth was. The whole thing was about the perception. It's like saying "Don't confuse me with reality because I know what the perception is." The capital fund argument made it look as if Adair were more expensive than PP&L. That was the point the county wanted to get across and they succeeded.

Unfortunately, a part of our rebuttal letter, which the newspapers focused on, was a remark we had made complaining that Adair Village was tired of being used as the "whipping boy" for Benton County. I know that we shouldn't have written that. It was not professional. But we felt it was true and had vented our frustration. We felt that we were wrongfully blamed for failure to finalize a contract proposal with North Albany.

I demanded an apology and a retraction of Blair's inaccurate estimate. The commissioners denied the need for an apology and Barbara Ross told James Blair to recheck his figures. Blair soon reported that his estimates were correct and that no retraction was necessary. Commissioner Ross said there was no reason for him to apologize for anything.

Many issues, conflicts, circumstances and opinions influenced this controversy. We may never know the real truth about why we were prevented from achieving a successful negotiation with North Albany. Benton County refused to endorse every water service contract proposal we successfully made, then said our failed negotiations proved we were unreliable. They stalled on the deadline for our bond election. They tried everything to get Eddie Hoops to change his mind. But, through all of this wrangling, Eddie stood by us. He continually believed in our determination to uphold our right of ownership. He gave us advice all along to stick to our guns. He saw the benefits the water plant held for our little city, and he shared our hopes for a bright economic future. With his support we received and maintained possession of the water and sewer plants and the valuable water rights. I am proud of that accomplishment!

Charline: We had this huge amount of water. So we approached the outlying water districts of North Albany.

Judi: You were fighting against huge odds. They were not about to let you service North Albany. It certainly would have helped our people here in Adair Village.

Charline: I spoke to the water boards and to any of the citizens who were there about how we could supply wholesale water to them at less than what PP&L would charge them.

Wanda: We made a real effort to be able to provide them with water. And Dumbeck was the only one who actually went with us for their water.

Charline: All of them were interested in our proposals until Jim Blair got involved with PP&L. He had supported us at first, but then said a lot of things that weren't true. The people were afraid to trust us. They believed we would not be able to run the plants, that they would be reverted from us.

Charline: Jim Blair painted the picture that it was a very unstable situation here. He spread the idea that if the water districts signed on with us it would likely not last. I heard it. When you are in the political world you hear it, a little bit here and a little bit there.

Judi: Look at it from an outsider's perspective. Here is the county engineer, Jim Blair, and he should KNOW. That is his business. The County Commissioners were the hot shots, the bosses, the leaders, and they said Adair would not be able to handle it. And here is little Adair, which really is brand new and what do we know?

Charline: The county engineer discounted what we said and he was the expert. You can see why people gave into that. It took real renegades, I can tell you, to go up against the county.

Delores: Would you consider yourself a renegade, Charline?

Charline: Yes, of course.

Wanda: I think we all were at that time.

Chapter 13: Conclusion

Back in the fall of 1978, we didn't fully realize how important it was for us to expand our water service area. I'm sorry we weren't able to make a contract with North Albany. I feel that we did everything we could to make that contract happen, but we were also caught up in getting the plants running. We were busy with the other hook-ups, even while working on getting the procurement building, and working on urban growth boundary decisions, plus all of the regular city business we had to attend to. We didn't realize the long-term effect that failure to acquire North Albany would have on Adair's economical progress. It is easy to look back and say this, but it may not be true. Who knows what problems might have prevented further success. The North Albany water service districts that were against Adair receiving the plants from HEW were the ones who wanted the plant themselves and were most adamant about not connecting up with us later that year. They probably would have continued to oppose us in any way they could.

The first water service from wells in North Albany had been formed there in 1930. I believe they felt entitled to the plant because of this history. It explains the angry outbursts toward Eddie when he gave the water plant and its systems to us, rather than to them. Indeed, they were the ones who received water service first from PP&L in late 1979. Afterwards, the annexation boundaries were revised and parts of North Albany, along with this water service district, were incorporated into Albany in 1981, three years later.

In 1991, voters approved annexation for the rest of the land inside the urban growth boundary, which formed what is now known as the North Albany District of Albany.

Life would have changed if we had become a water supplier for North Albany. We would have had considerably more money, simply because of the increased number of customers. It would have been a larger operation. We might have been using more of the plant so we would have definitely had to hire more public works staff. I think the plant would have been totally refurbished, if not rebuilt, by now. Our relationship with our neighbors might have been better, more cooperative. I think there might have been a greater sense of community in North Benton County. North Albany has changed considerably. It has grown from 1,500 to around 8,000 people now. Our population has grown from 550 to around 1,000. Most of the people who were involved in all of the water controversy are gone. I know a few people who live in North Albany but not many, and they are not the old timers who lived through the water controversy.

Adair Village is a unique city in many ways. It is hard to find other small cities that have the same problems that we do. I wonder if we had taken a different direction, decided to sell water rights to another entity, we may not have had to struggle financially as we have. We would like to have a downtown and some of the services that other small cities enjoy, like a library, a bigger grocery store, service station, and those kinds of things. We have not been able to do it because of lack of money, and I wonder if we had sold some of the water rights, things would have been financially better for us.

To keep the city from bankruptcy, we had to raise the water rates in 2000. For many years, the council that was sitting didn't want to do that. The cost of making water went up and up but what people paid for it stayed the same. Eventually, we had to make the hard decision and do it. We explained why so many years went by without a rate change and we had to make up for that. The citizens accepted it, didn't like it, but accepted it. We didn't really have a choice.

Retaining the water rights has become increasingly more and more difficult to justify. Those rights are old and valuable. We had some regulation in the past but nothing like what we have now. It used to be a fairly simple thing. We would send a letter to the Department of Water Resources once every five years.

The city is working on a new water plan. We are seeking grants and funding resources to replace the existing plant, the holding tanks, pump stations and pipes. Water plants are very small and high tech these days. One of the new ones could be built on the land we own at the current water plant.

When Dumbeck water district left Adair to hook up to the Albany water system in 2007, there was some discussion about Albany possibly connecting up to the Adair water plant, sometime in the future. We could serve as an emergency back-up system if something happened to North Albany's water supply from the Lyons Street Bridge pipe or the Santiam River. The city has some big plans in play right now, and they are working their way through, step by step, to take care of these things. The likelihood is that City of Adair Village may someday become a water supplier for the mid-valley region. The potential is there.

Gazette Times

On the walkway of the water plant with the valve wheel.

Part 3:
City
Particulars

The City of Adair Village

City Government

The Mayor/Council

The mayor/council is the oldest form of city government in the United States and, until the beginning of the 20th century, was used by nearly all American cities. Adair's city government has an elected council of five members, including the mayor, who has certain executive powers.

Adair Village Mayors (in the order served):
Charline (Carr) King
Ted Cain
Jim Ableman
Charline (Carr) King
R. C. Widony
Craig Bartlett
Faye Abraham
Bob Thayer
Bill Currier

The mayor appoints members of city departments and other officials, with the approval of the council. The mayor and council conduct city business by majority vote to pass city ordinances, apportion money among the various city departments and address community concerns. They also approve or reject recommendations from the Planning and Budget Committee, the two most important committees.

The City Administrator

This position was created for the complexity of problems that need management ability not often possessed by elected public officials. An elected council makes the city ordinances and sets policy, but hires a skilled paid administrator to carry out its decisions. He or she draws up the city budget and supervises most of the personnel and activity of the city's departments. There is no set term.

Wanda Tobiassen

Served from 1976-2000

Wanda was the first Adair Village City Administrator. She served in that position from 1976 until she retired after 24. She then worked four years for the city of Sheridan before retiring from that job in 2004.

Besides the water plant acquisition and all that entailed, Wanda worked to meet the state guidelines for land use planning. The city council applied for a Comprehensive Land Use grant that would move up the completion of the Comprehensive Plan from March 1983 to March 1981. The grant was for a one-year total cost of $9,000 from the LCDC (Land Conservation and Development Commission) with the city supplying 10% from in-kind services. Adair Village was so small, it didn't have some of the problems addressed, but we still had to work through them just as though we were a larger city. That is where our city planner Don Driscoll came in. He guided us through the process. The comprehensive land use plan and land use development code are extremely important in how we develop as a city.

Gazette Times

Office Assistant Lynn O'Brian (standing) and Adair City Administrator Wanda Tobiassen (sitting) working together in the city office in 1985.

Wanda remembers moving into the city offices in the Community Building in 1980. Soon after that move, the city received their first computer. Lynn O'Brian, Wanda's assistant, said her uncle Chuck offered them computer tutorials. So, Lynn and Wanda flew to California for three days and learned how to use the computer for city business. The computer was a gift from Uncle Chuck who mailed an enormous computer to the city office.

I had never held a city recorder's job before, so I relied on our attorney and auditor for guidance in setting up the necessary internal functions of a city office. I was appointed as budget officer. The budget committee, city auditor, and I set up the city budget.

Wanda remembers the planning commission as an important part of the growth and progress of the city. They dealt with neighborhood issues, such as painting the houses and duplexes. They even addressed restrictions such as the owner of one side wanting it painted one color and the owner of the other side wanting it painted a different color. Decisions made about what some people wanted affected the rest of the community. The zero lot line zoning was put into place, which allowed people to buy half a duplex, rather than the whole thing. The planning commission drew up plans for the urban growth boundary and formulated the plans and restrictions for expansion and future development.

Wanda

The city planner for Corvallis called me one day and said that Adair needed to change the name of Willamette Street because Corvallis was getting a Willamette Street. I said, "No, we had ours first, and as long as I am here, we are not changing it." We were very brave. There is another Azalea Street in Corvallis, as well, but ours in Adair is Azalea Drive.

Starting this city and succeeding took a leap of faith, a lot of communication, dedication, and hard work. Charline was elected as a county commissioner and submitted her resignation as mayor in November of 1980. I kept her in touch with what was happening during the eight years she served on the Board of Commissioners. She rejoined the council when her second term was completed in 1988.

Charline

Wanda stepped in to cover as Adair City Administrator in 2007 after Jim Minard left. She served for six months prior to the hiring of Drew Foster. Our friendship flourished during those years working together to start the city and we are bonded for life. Not a week goes by that we are not in contact with each other, having lunch or just talking on the phone.

Robert (Bob) King

Served from April to August 2000

As a resident of the City of Adair Village, Bob volunteered to work as city administrator for a six-month period following Wanda's retirement in 2000. Prior to this, Bob served as city administrator for the City of Turner, Oregon, retiring from that position after nine years. Bob accepted the temporary job with Adair Village for no pay, choosing to receive recompense in water and sewer service for several months, instead. He helped make the tough decision to raise the utility rates and helped the city face some tough times with water losses.

Delores Pollard

A nice place to stroll under oak trees on Arnold Avenue.

Jim Minard

Served from 2000-2007

Jim was hired August 2000 and served as City Administrator until leaving the position in April 2007. Minard worked 35 hours a week and also acted as the City Planner. Before becoming Adair Village's city administrator, Minard was an associate planner with Benton County from 1995 to 1999. During Minard's seven years as an administrator, the city's financial stability improved. He helped lead growth efforts that most residents supported. Minard contracted with an outside firm to provide public works services and helped create the new community building after the old one was damaged in a summer fire in 2004.

Delores Pollard

The city council met in Laborers Trust cafeteria after the fire.

Drew Foster

Served from 2007-2015

Drew was City Administrator from October 2007 until he retired in July 2015. He received a Masters of Public Administration from the University of Oregon. During the twelve years prior to coming to Adair Village, he worked for the Oregon Cascades West Council of Governments as a community development planner/regional investment program coordinator. Drew was instrumental in many things. He was extremely valuable to the city in the utilization of his professional organizational planning skills. Drew analyzed and stabilized much of the groundwork necessary for our continued growth and development. This work included updating our city's comprehensive land use plan as well as the SDC (System Development Charges), which establish the necessary standards for effective continual growth. Thanks to Drew's efforts, along with Mayor Bill Currier and Mayor Pro Tem Charline King, our city and financial policies are firmly in place. Drew had the ability to step into a difficult situation and leave it with everyone thinking of him as a great guy. People really liked him.

Pat Hare

Serving from 2015- Current

Pat Hare started working for the City of Adair Village as an intern in 2010. He spent the first two weeks looking into the maps and utility billing information of water loss in the city. The next two weeks he worked finding the actual location of the water lines, most of which did not exist as shown on the maps. After this 30-day internship ended, Pat was contracted to continue work on the water line project for another year while he finished his bachelor's degree at Western Oregon University. In July of 2011, Pat was offered an Assistant City Administrator position, which he held for two years and eight months while getting his Master's Degree in the PPPM Program, (Planning, Public Policy and Management) at University of Oregon. In 2012, the city decided to bring Public Works in-house again and they hired Pat to run it. He hired Tom Shaddon and together they worked hard to find the big leaks and cut the water loss in half.

Over the next five years, under Pat's guidance, Adair Village can expect to see some innovative ideas come to fruition. In addition to water conservation and management, we hope to see progress made in business development, housing and infrastructure.

"To be honest," Pat begins, "the decision to become a city administrator didn't come until Adair Village offered me a job. I was almost finished with my internship at Adair Village and I was looking for employment in the public works field somewhere. I applied for a public works supervisor position in Metolius, Oregon and shortly after applying I received a call for an interview. I told the city officials of Adair Village about the interview. A few days later Drew Foster, the City Administrator told me that if I decided to stay, they would make me the Assistant City Administrator. It wasn't until that moment that I decided to head down this career path."

Judi

People are not educated about paying taxes. They do not understand what a privilege it is. What we get from our taxes is really phenomenal. We see a lot of benefits like infrastructure, roads, etc., and we get back a lot for what we pay. I pay my tax money to help all of us.

Delores

We take things for granted, like a city's infrastructure. My father was a Sea Bee in WWII. He built roads in the Philippines. He taught me to appreciate roads and bridges. We'd drive out to the wilderness and he'd say, "This is how it was when the pioneers had to struggle across the land. Now, we can drive safely through it."

Charline

When I first became mayor in 1976, our city budget was about $20,000 a year. I remember publicly remarking that I did not believe we would ever need more than that. In 2015, the city budget is over $2 million. We should really have a tax rate higher than we do, but there is no way to raise it in this economic climate. Nobody is going to be willing to vote for that, but someday we may need to have it on the ballot.

Delores Pollard

Dramatic bare trees in late fall reveal the Community Building.

The Procurement Building

"Where, Of Course, Can The Council Be?"
read the 1976 newspaper headline. We had no money to
buy or build a city hall and we desperately needed a
place to meet and to store city records. Wanda, as the
city recorder, was keeping the city file cabinets in her
home. Oregon State Law required that city councils
meet within city limits, but we owned no property and
no building. We had been operating as a city for seven
months and meeting in the CISCO cafeteria. After they
closed, we met in different rooms of Sweathouse Lodge.
The Sweathouse Lodge was an alcohol rehabilitation

program for Native Americans, which remained as a separate rehabilitation center when CISCO closed.

We moved around and met in a dormitory, or the conference room, or the kitchen. Sweathouse Lodge didn't last long, although they stayed on the property for 18 months after the property and buildings were sold to the Laborers Trust. After that, the city council met in the Laborers Trust building, room 232, for a short while. The Laborers Trust wanted to expand its carpentry-training program. They approached our city council and asked us to re-zone the property to educational. I am glad we did that then, as it served us well later on when Santiam Christian School applied for the property and it was already zoned educational.

We sent an application to GSA (General Services Administration) in early 1977, for the dining hall, which had been the Non-commissioned Officers' Club building. GSA thought it was best suited for our use as a city hall because the building could easily be separated from either a purchase or a grant of the remaining property. We really wanted it. They wanted to give it to us but had to go through their legal process. If another government agency or school wanted it, they had to apply for it and then buy it. All these other people had first chance. Then, if nobody else bought it, they could give it to us. The building would cost about $70,000 with the needed repairs. Wanda set about seeking grants available to small cities for such needs.

We, as the council, wrote to Oregon Senators Mark Hatfield and Bob Packwood and to Representative Les AuCoin and to President Carter, seeking help to get our building. Senator Hatfield was the only one to answer and he referred us to GSA, which did not help any as we had already been there. That tells me two things. We were gutsy enough to go to Senator Hatfield and President Carter, but we didn't get much help from them. Money was tight in those days for everyone, and some of the local criticism was against us in that regard. Some people said the building should be given to an agency that could create jobs in Adair Village and who could contribute to the tax base. They thought we should levy a city tax to be able to pay for our own city hall.

In September of 1977, I had a conversation with Bill Chapman, of the Benton County Parks and Recreation Department. He came to our next city council meeting and talked to us concerning the possibility of getting the old procurement building on the strip of land east of Highway 99W, instead of the NCO Club. The county had no plans to use the building or the property at that time. Dan Callahan, chairman of the city hall committee, and I attended the next Parks Board meeting, on February 7, 1978. The County voted unanimously to allow the procurement building to revert to GSA with the recommendation that we be given first option. Then Dan moved away. Mary (Phillips) Wright took over the responsibilities of the application for the building with GSA. That is the way it was with us. If something needed to be done and the person could not do it for some reason, another one of us stepped in. Of course we had disagreements, as all groups do who work closely together, but in the end, we always had each other's backs and everyone worked very hard.

GSA would give us the building free of cost on condition that we repair and maintain it. The building was beginning to have water damage on the floors and needed a new roof. Mary spent many long, cold hours that winter taking pictures of the damage and getting estimates for the repair. It cost about $15,000.

We also received a triangle piece of land with the building amounting to 3.3 acres, adjacent to 99W. Originally, the county had the idea to make it a roadside rest area. Mary drew up the plans for the park area, necessary for the application, suggesting spots for picnic benches, a horseshoe pit and possible landscape elements in the city park.

Hank Dickerson wrote to Senator Mark Hatfield asking his support in helping Adair Village get the building. Whether this had anything to do with the ultimate outcome or not, I don't know. But our lawyer worked hard and always had our backs, too.

Gazette Times

Councilmember Jim Ableman and his daughter often visited the library room in the Community Building.

The deed for the city hall building was signed in October 1978. Receiving the procurement building was a happy and hopeful moment. We now had the office and the meeting space for the big change that was coming: the water contract with North Albany. Everything seemed to be falling in place for us.

After we acquired the building, we contracted the Willamette Carpenter School to help with repairs. They started work on the roof in February of 1979. One of the stipulations of receiving the building was that we had to put up a sign within six months saying the building and property was a recreational area that had been given by the federal government. We allotted $250 for this sign. Because the property came from the government, we could never call it a city hall. We could have called it The City of Adair Village Parks Building, if we had wanted. We had to keep it open for public use and so we called it the Community Building.

Most of the money we used to fix it up came from donations. Wanda had four boys who were earning their Boy Scouts' Eagle rank. The boys' projects included work on the grounds, the parking lot and the front steps. It was wonderful. We had to pay for materials but we didn't need a lot. The ceiling in the procurement building had come down because of the rain, but most of what was needed was labor.

The Corvallis post office suggested that we change the name of the street where the Community Building was, since it was named First Street on the maps and there already was a First Street in Corvallis. We voted to change the name to Columbia Avenue by simply extending the existing Columbia Avenue south from the corner at Arnold Avenue to Vandenberg. The Community Building became 103 Columbia Avenue.

We used the building for the first time for a city council meeting on April 16, 1979, two years and 11 months after Adair Village became a city. The building was hardly ready. The south windows were leaning against the wall ready to be installed. The interior ceiling wasn't finished, and there were no light fixtures. There were outlets, though. Wanda and I brought lamps from our homes and plugged them in so that we had light for our meeting. I can just see us in that big dark building huddled together around a circle of light, happily having our first official city council meeting in our own official building.

Charline	We had one room that was designated a library and it was really nice. People could check out books and return them.
Wanda	One of our first librarians, Debbie Bailey, had kids. In the wintertime, because the library room was cold, she would bring the baby into my office and we would put the baby next to the heater. She was a good librarian, too. She was always having little parties and activities for the kids that were here. We often had a whole room full of kids. She did a great job.
Charline	Debbie lived down by my house on the lower loop. When she was pregnant she took walks every morning and she waddled past my house on her walks. "Hi. Debbie." "Hi, Charline," every day. I can just see her.

It's too bad we lost that old building to the fire in 2004. Some remodeling was being planned to make it usable for what we needed, but what I thought important was the fact that it was one of the very last remaining Camp Adair buildings. It could have had offices and storage closets added. There was plenty of room. There was that BIG room. The remodeling plans showed a counter where people could pay their utility bills. The north side would have had a normal sized room, and it would have taken up a very small percentage of that huge room. We sure had some nice parties in there. We had food brought in for community potlucks along with music and dances. The big kitchen was great.

Delores Pollard

The Community Building houses the City Hall 2015.

I don't know what the Air Force used it for, but the original procurement building was a non-denominational church for the post WWII GI Bill veterans. When I lived here as a kid, I remember we used to find a way in and go around in there and push each other on chairs. I slipped and got a bloody nose par excellence and they had to take me home.

I have one copy of their *Village Spirit* church newsletter. There is an article about my mother in there, who started the Sunday school at the church. They gave her a commendation for her service.

The chapels were not at this end of Camp Adair. This end was the hospital. The Air Force flattened most of it. The Air Force buildings are the historical sites now, though we have 6 original old camp structures left: The store, the two barracks, the four-plex, the ordinance building and the smokestack.

To see the story of the churches go to Gary L. Richard's site http://campadair.webs.com

What Are We Doing Now?

A water plant repair report from 2012 from Garret Pallo our engineer at Civil West Engineering Services Inc., to the Adair Village City Council:

"The work is done. The plant is back on line. The flocculate system is turning smoothly, the leakage is stopped and the surface wash system is fully functional. They were able to finish the work a little earlier than estimated, which is great news. It turns out they ran into a number of pretty significant tank problems once they started to rework the paddles and axels. Previous projects of workmanship had things out of alignment, which contributed to the leakage by placing stress on the bearings and penetrations. They did all they could, given the short time frame to correct these issues and put it back together in almost like new condition.

This improvement will last many, many years and help the city by buying you time while you address other issues and prepare to undertake a new water plant many years down the road when times are more appropriate. While we cannot say for sure, we believe the plant was approaching a major breakdown that would have made water production nearly impossible.

"The city public works department, particularly Pat (Hare) and Tom (Shaddon), should be commended for their efforts this past year. The fact that you are able to be down for four or five or more days is a testament to the success you have had in reducing leakage to the system. Not long ago it was difficult to talk about having the plant off-line for only one or two days. This is clear evidence of your successes and accomplishments. While this project has cost more than you had hoped and planned it was the right thing to do and it will pay many dividends to the city by having a reliable plant. Thanks to the folks at Koonts Machinery for their hard work and long hours. The truth is, we did not know just how bad the problems were until the contractors started tearing things apart and seeing for themselves. It is the nature of a remodel that problems and required work reveals itself after the work and the associated budget are committed."

The wonderful thing about that report was that he said this improvement would last "many, many years down the road!" The other thing is that we went four or five days without operating the water plant and did not run out of water. That shows we caught most of the leaks.

Wanda

One time my assistant and I were working up in the yard right by the water plant. The ground was wet and we could tell there was a leak. We had a backhoe and he dug to the pipe. He was drinking a Pepsi. I said, "When you get done with that, let me have the bottle." So, he did and I wrote a note, which told what we were doing on this water line and who we were. I put the date on it and we buried it there.

Judi

A time capsule!

In 2010, there was a hot, hot spell. We were never quite out of water with the Voss Hill reservoir, up on the hill along Independence Highway, but it came very close. Our public works staff was quite new then because we had just ended our contract with an outside provider and had established our own public works department again. They were working seven days a week, 24 hours a day to keep us in water. If the hot spell had lasted any longer we probably would not have had water. We could not shut the plant down at all, and now we can shut it down for four to five days.

System repairs have cut our water loss from over 60 % to somewhere down around 40%. We are getting a loan to install two new, expandable steel water tanks on Voss Hill. It is estimated that when the new reservoirs are built and the old Voss Hill reservoir is shut down, we will probably have a water loss of somewhere around 20%. Voss Hill reservoir is so old it is like a sieve. It is made of cement and most of it is underground so you can't see where it is leaking.

Another large repair in the old system was what we called the Hospital Hill Rehabilitation. Hospital Hill Reservoir is on top of the hill across 99W from the city. It pumped water to Calloway and Arbor Springs Estates. About 15 years ago they had to drain it, patch it and reline it. There were leaks that were hard to find that drained down through the forest. Those repairs worked for a number of years but Hospital Hill reservoir has now been taken off line because of more leaks.

It is hard to know where the old lines are. We don't have a real map of where all of the meters and valves and other things are for the old lines, especially the big one that goes to the north. So, when a leak developed there, it took them forever to find it. There was a gigantic leak, hundreds of gallons a minute. Our people couldn't find the line except that they noticed 20-

30 foot high trees growing in a straight line, which was a clue there was water there! Isn't that wonderful. And they didn't even know where the valve was to turn the water off for that line because when it came out of Voss Hill it didn't come out in the direction they anticipated. There was a little extra turn in there. Those were all little steps, little mysteries, to solve water leakage problems.

The old pipes have been replaced up north going to Camp Adair Road where the Fish and Wildlife properties are. Originally there was an eight-inch main serving the cantonment, which was a huge line. We put in a two-inch pipeline that will last for years for people out that way. The ongoing water loss is part of the reason why the water rates have gone up. We just can't afford to keep on pouring treated water out somewhere. Treated water is expensive.

> Judi
>
> Charline, you laid the groundwork but you hadn't seen the fruits. Your efforts, the way you organized, the people you approached, bore fruit after you left the mayorship for your commissioner duties with the county.

We do supply water to quite a large region now. There are customers along Independence Road and some on Tampico Road. There are some along Arboretum Road. South of Ryals Lane on Logsdon Ridge there are people who have agreed to put in water lines and receive water from us. They have to provide the lines from Voss Hill to their places.

When that plant was built during World War II, I don't think that saving water was their big concern. At that time it was a very up-to-date water plant. When the camp was operating, Voss Hill held a million gallons of water and Hospital Hill held half a million. A reservoir on Coffin Butte held another half a million. At Camp Adair in the early 40's, the water plant was serving at least 50,000 people at any one time. It went from serving 50,000 down to 550, plus these outlying hook-ups. We reduced some of the equipment in the plant to make it smaller because the cost to run a plant with that capacity was so huge. It was so expensive, that we cut down the operation. There are six holding tanks where the finished water goes and we are using only three of them, so it is less expensive for us to operate. There was also an underground holding tank for finished water that we don't use. The good thing is, we don't have to operate it all day and all night to have drinking water.

There are many tests we have to do on the water at the water plant, and on the water at the sewer plant, to meet the state standards. It takes a lot of documentation to operate those old plants: the daily chlorine, how many chemicals were added, the turbidity tests and where they were taken, and the daily log of what our operators do. There are about five or six different things to do everyday to have the plant running. Those guys are awfully busy when they are out there, and the forms are all filled in by hand.

It is much more technical now than it used to be. In our plant it is still hands-on. Some operational changes have been made, but some of it is still done the old way. Finding qualified operators is a challenge because they no longer teach how to operate the old plants. Every once in awhile something fails and we get a notice from the state that says we are being fined because we are not in compliance with the state laws and regulations.

Wanda: In the early 1990's we were replacing some things in the water plant. I remember seeing some of those unused holding tanks and there was a tree growing up out of one of them.

Judi: There were rocks and sand in there for filtering the water. Every once in awhile we had to change the rocks and get new cleaned sand.

Wanda: I was up at the water plant one day and spotted a little fish swimming around in a water-settling tank there. I asked the operators, "How did this little fish get all the way up here from the Willamette? He is not supposed to be here." So we had to get a diver to go down into the river and check the intakes. And sure enough there were holes that had been worn into the screen.

Judi: And after the boat ramp was put in there, it changed the way the currents drop the sand. We have to periodically dredge it out.

City Signs Through Time

Gazette Times

The Air Force Station in 1957 built two stone signs, one on each side of the main entrance. The platforms for both of these signs still exist and have since become garden beds. The redwood and western red cedar trees across the road behind this sign are still small.

You can see the backs of some of the newly built duplexes on the Willamette Street upper loop. The SAGE building is not visible, being off to the right. The oak tree on the right is an identifying marker in many of the old Adair pictures.

The Commuter - Linn Benton Community College

This was the first city sign created in 1976 soon after the city was incorporated. Wanda remembers that it was dark brown with gold letters and a gold wheat emblem in a square.

Again, we can see the oak tree in the background and the clump of red cedars and redwoods. This sign was on the south side of the Arnold Avenue entrance, near where the present sign stands now in 2016.

Delores Pollard

This sky-blue hand painted sign was put up sometime around the year 2000. It stood until 2010 when a resident accidently missed the curve toward the stop sign and drove off the road and destroyed it. The flowerbox is built on the cement remnant of the Air Force station sign.

The hawthorn tree to the left is one of a number of them spaced along William R. Carr to the north. They have bright red berries that last through the winter. Also, to the north there is one beautiful madrone tree along with a variety of pines. Madrone trees furnish food for some types of butterflies.

The stop sign seems to have been there forever. It is in many pictures of the early Air Force station days.

Delores Pollard

The present entry sign stands on the right hand side of the entrance to the west of the old Air Force station cement pad. It has the city motto written in metal script: Grounded in history, growing for the future. The sign was finished in 2012. Students and staff from Santiam Christian School's agriculture classes completed the final landscaping and irrigation.

The city council sent out a call for designs and took them to a designer in Eugene. This sign was created as a class project with the assistance of the University of Oregon's Resource Assistance for Rural Environments (RARE) program. This organization offers creative approaches to downtown revitalization through strong leadership that results in significant, long-term contributions.

The Barricade

Some people who lived on Azalea Drive found a short cut home by driving straight across the empty field off Columbia Avenue, (which is now William R. Carr Avenue). They used the empty field for extra parking for visitors in the summers and to unload long firewood timber to cut up in the fall. But Lorraine Ruff, who lived there on the corner of Columbia, objected to that. She began complaining about what she called the Adair Village Freeway. Lorraine contacted the State Highway Department one August and requested that a safety barrier be built there, telling them that cars occasionally slid off the road when it was icy. The Highway Department agreed that a fence would add to the safety of the road. So Bill Carr and a couple of other fellows built a fence to keep people from driving through the field. It was a wooden barrier with a 2x6 rail that was painted white. The interesting thing about that was the fact that two of the couples who lived along there were Jim and Mo Ableman, and Mary and Chuck Phillips. Both Jim and Chuck were on the city council and Mary was on the planning commission and all were close friends of ours.

Gazette Times.

The wooden barrier seen in 1979 at Columbia Avenue corner.

The *Gazette Times* read: "Affected Councilmen Vote to Remove Adair Barrier," The affected councilmen were, of course, both Chuck and Jim. But Lorraine, always the political activist, went around collecting names in support of her petition to stop the traffic across the field. Fifty-eight citizens signed the petition to keep the $700 barrier in place. At a council meeting the city lawyer explained that if there were an accident on the corner, the city would face more liability if the fence were removed. The vote was three in favor of keeping it up, against two to take it down. The next news headline read: "Adair Council Reverses Vote. Barrier to Stay Up."

The contention ended at this point. There could have been another petition made to take the barrier down, but no one did it. The councilmembers either drove around the end of the barrier, or took the Azalea loop to get to the front of their homes. They were not too happy about that, which was understandable, especially when you consider how parking is at such a premium on our narrow streets. Anyway, the councilmembers called it The Bill Carr Barricade for years.

The barricade was eventually removed when we built the Castle Lands subdivision on that city-annexed property along the backyards. William R. Carr Avenue was extended down to the corner where Barberry Drive turns to the east into the extended subdivision.

Delores Pollard

Beyond the Bill Carr Barricade. William R. Carr Avenue is the main entrance to the subdivision on the north side of the city.

Delores: What about the dark cloud on the city council? I found a stack of little newspaper stories about an Adair Village couple getting caught shoplifting.

Charline: Oh, you've run across that, have you?

Delores: How embarrassing that must have been!

Judi: We weren't going to say anything about that!

Wanda: I was going to leave those at home and not give them to you.

Judi: Shall we just…burn the building?

Charline: I suppose you want to know how that happened?

Delores: No. Not really. I think I know how that happened. Adair Village had some homes that flooded. Since these people were shoplifting household repair items, I assumed they needed something desperately to repair the water damage.

Wanda: It was when the water heaters exploded.

Charline: So, you want to know about that couple's situation?

Delores: Well, not if you don't want to tell me. And that's fine. It can be a secret buried in history that nobody has to know.

Charline: But just in the matter of interest...

Delores

Okay! Okay, then Charline...go ahead and tell me. You're the boss.

Charline

Wanda and I read in the paper that one of our councilmembers and his wife had been arrested for shoplifting. I don't remember what their punishment was.

Judi

They had ten days probation. It wasn't grand larceny...it was $41.00 (well, inflation would make it around $200 today.) They didn't go to jail or anything.

Charline

It was a complete shock to us. We were trying hard to make a good name for Adair Village and this was just awful. We thought people might say, "You know, Adair Village, where that guy on the city council was caught shoplifting?" Wanda and I talked about it at great length. We were just sick about it. It was a black smear against the city, with him being on the council.

Wanda

We were well aware of what a black mark that was against the city. That's the thing. They were involved in the city and they did essential work for years, and yet they did this stupid thing.

Judi: Well, there were other kinds of stupid things that happened.

Wanda: That's true.

Delores Pollard

One of the new houses in the subdivision on Barberry Drive.

The Barracks

Gazette Times

These old barracks were severely weathered and in need of repair. They are two of the few remaining old Camp Adair buildings.

In March 2010, the city saved two World War II buildings and moved them to the north end of the city park. The buildings were donated to the city by Santiam Christian School. The city set them on foundations and put on new roofs, new siding and new windows. Plumbing and wiring were done, but the interiors of the buildings were not finished. The city plans to turn one of the buildings into a community center. There are plans for the second building to create an interpretative history center about Camp Adair.

> **Charline**
>
> I'm thrilled and delighted. I love the historical aspect of this project. I am very much in love with what Adair Village was, is and will become.

Later in 2010, Barbara Melton and a group of civic-minded Adair Village residents founded Adair Living History Inc. (ALH), an incorporated non-profit entity separate from the city. Their mission is to complete its Raise the Barracks project. The end of one building will depict the interior environment of the original soldiers' quarters. In 2016, ALH received grants and donations to begin ADA compliant renovation of the entryways. Future plans include complete restoration for multiple uses. There will be space for community activities and historical displays for tourists and visitors. If you wish to donate to this restoration project, send tax-deductible donations to Adair Living History Inc. at 176 NE Azalea Drive, Adair Village OR, 97330 or donate online at adairlivinghistory.org.

Delores Pollard

The barracks at the city park in 2016 with work underway.

Part 4:
Persons and Places of Interest

Judith Vedamuthu
1941-2014

Judith (Judi) Ann Hoeye Vedamuthu, daughter, sister, wife and mother, was born to Wyman Delos Hoeye and Virginia Ellen Mason Hoeye on June 14, 1941, in Longview, Washington.

When her father enlisted in the U.S. Army, Judi and her mother moved to Mill City to live with Judi's grandmother, Edith Mason, a librarian at Mill City High School (now Santiam Union High School). When Judi's father completed his tour of duty with the Army, the family moved to Adair Village Student Housing where he finished a degree in industrial arts at Oregon State University, and taught industrial arts at Mill City High.

They returned to Mill City, where Judi graduated from high school in 1959. With the family moving to Corvallis, Judi continued her education at OSU, where she met Ebenezer (Eb) Rajkumar Vedamuthu, a doctoral student in microbiology from Madras (now Chennai), India. They were married on Aug. 17, 1963.

The couple followed Eb's career to Ames, Iowa, where he worked at Iowa State University, and where their first son, Jonathan Jeyakaran, was born. They then moved to Bradenton, Florida, where their second son, Daniel Savarirayan, was born. Their final career move was to Rochester, Minnesota, where Eb retired from Quest International in 2000. On retiring, Judi and Eb moved back to Oregon in 2001. Judi followed her passion for learning and libraries in every place they lived, working for the OSU Library soon after her marriage, and then working for the Manatee Public Library in Bradenton before becoming the librarian at St. Stephen's Episcopal School. She worked as an archivist for the City of Adair until her death.

Judi also remained deeply devoted to the faith she shared with her husband, and she studied the Scripture intensively and served in various capacities for the Methodist Church, lastly at College United Methodist Church in Philomath.

Judi will be remembered for her generosity of spirit, her warm smile, her quick mind, her cheerful demeanor and her great energy. She valiantly fought against cancer for six years, leading all who knew her to believe she would conquer it. She died the night of March 18, 2014, at Samaritan Evergreen Hospice House in Albany. She was a delightful and loving addition to our Adair Diary writing project. We miss her very much.

George E. (Eddie) Hoops
1936-1995

The Seattle Times By E.J.Gong Jr. Copyright (c) 1995 *Seattle Times* Company, All Rights Reserved.

"George E. Hoops, 59, Loved Family, Cooking, Hunting Everybody called him "Fast Eddie" because he never stood still. If George Edward Hoops wasn't salmon fishing, deer hunting or barbecuing, he was telling jokes or cradling his grandson.

"My father had a real zest for life," said Stephanie Hoops, 26, of Kirkland. ""He loved to cook, he loved the outdoors, and he loved his family and friends."

Mr. Hoops, 59, who died from a heart attack on June 9 while mowing the lawn at his Bellevue home, enjoyed a wide range of interests that he worked hard to perfect.

Mr. Hoops was an award-winning barbecue chef. Mr. Hoops - along with his wife, Wanda, and another couple - won first prize in the Pig War Barbecue contest in Friday Harbor. That victory qualified the barbecuing team, called the Sow Bellies, for a chance to compete in an international event in Canada.

"Eddie had a secret sauce with a secret ingredient which won us many awards," said Lee Wakefield, a close friend and member of the barbecue team. "He later told me the secret ingredient was Jack Daniels!"

"Eddie also was a great shot. He loved to hunt for elk and deer throughout the state," said Wakefield, a retired Minnesota police officer who met Mr. Hoops in 1986.

Born in Kansas City, Kan., Mr. Hoops served in the Navy during the Korean War. Afterward, he took a job with the U.S. Department of Education, where he was in charge of transferring surplus government property to educational institutions.

Mr. Hoops was responsible for property from the western banks of the Mississippi River to Guam, said David Hakola, Mr. Hoops' supervisor in Washington, D.C. "Eddie was a walking fountain of knowledge. With nearly 40 years of experience, what he could do in five minutes would take me all day," Hakola said.

Mr. Hoops handled the transfer of federal property to the Pacific Science Center at Seattle Center, Hakola said.

Mr. Hoops moved to Bellevue in 1970. For more than a decade, he also owned the Red Carpet Dry Cleaners in Bellevue and Redmond.

Three months ago, Wanda Hoops, Mr. Hoops' wife of 37 years, died from complications following heart surgery. The loss devastated Mr. Hoops, Stephanie Hoops said.

"My father and mother were deeply in love, and I think he couldn't live without her," Stephanie Hoops said. "I think my father died of a broken heart, but at least I know my parents are together."

Eddie came to town to settle a boundary complaint. The man filed an adverse **Judi** possession lawsuit. He had farmed the land to the point that the property post on one of the corners had been plowed under and he was going to move the new post onto the Adair water plant property. Eddie said, "I remember talking to that man and NO! He can't do that!" That put an end to it.

William (Bill) R. Carr
1923-1980

One recent Halloween I had 82 trick-or-treaters come to my door. Out of the shadows by my bushes some of the little kids' parents called to me, "Hello, Mrs. Carr! Remember me? These are *my* kids. I was here trick-or-treating when I was *their* age!" I told that story at the council meeting November of 2014 and a new member said, "You were Mrs. *Carr*? Then is that street named after your first husband?" I answered yes and another woman also new on the council said she didn't know that either. They had no clue that William R. Carr Avenue was named after a real person who did so much for this city, not someone from World War II Camp Adair or from the Air Force station.

When my husband Bill Carr died June third, 1980, I was still mayor, but, of course, I missed the next evening's council meeting. Councilor Chuck Phillips stopped by and told me they had named a street for Bill while I wasn't there. They changed the name of the long stretch of Columbia Avenue, to William R. Carr Avenue in honor of him. William R. Carr is important in connection with our early history. Bill did much for this city, before it was incorporated and after. He worked for the City of Albany and operated both the Adair water and sewer plants when they were still in possession of Albany. After Adair Village received the plants, Bill trained our operators. He had earned his certifications through a two-year program at Linn-Benton Community College when jobs for water and wastewater operators were a hot potato. It was a big thing then, but you had to have certifications and keep going back to keep them updated. It was unusual to have certifications in both water and sewer treatment, which Bill did, and that is why Albany hired him. He wrote the operation manuals for both the Adair water and sewer treatment plants. Bill Carr knew our water systems inside and out because he was the one who had been operating them for Albany since 1973.

When Bill first worked for Albany he was not a supervisor, and he was required to work rotating shifts. He worked a month on days from eight until four, then a month on swing shift from three until midnight and a month on night shift from midnight until eight. This went on for three years before he was promoted to Assistant Superintendent for the wastewater treatment plant for Albany. Then he went on straight days Monday through Friday. This seemed like Heaven to us! I had been attending Linn-Benton Community College during our first two years here, and with my classes and Bill's rotating shifts, we saw very little of each other.

Delores Pollard

North on William R. Carr before Carmen Place was finished.

At this time I was also managing five duplexes for Dr. Wilson, which were 10 living units. I kept them rented, screened potential renters and kept them up to Dr. Wilson's standards. But Bill was the one who did all the repairs. He was working full time for Albany, volunteering for Adair and also doing repair and maintenance for those 10 units.

Bill was not on the city council, though we had many meetings at our house around our dining room table. He would be there when he could, but he wasn't part of it. He was very supportive and wished the best for the city.

The Commuter – Linn Benton Community College

Bill and Charline Carr around 1976. Mary Wright shared a secret that Bill told her, " When I first laid eyes on Charline, I thought she was the most beautiful woman I had ever seen."

Bill was the first black firefighter for the city of Portland. This was years before I knew him. He was 29 years old then. That was quite an accomplishment in those days.

He was an avid reader. Bill could read and read and read. He had eidetic memory, where he could memorize things without trying. He could look at a page and then remember it. We read a lot of the same books. I remember one time I said, "Bill, there is no way you can read a book so fast and remember what you are reading." He said, "Yes. I can. Pick a page and ask me." So I randomly picked a page and said, "Okay, page 121." And he proceeded to tell me what was on it! Bill read an entire encyclopedia when he was twelve years old, all of the volumes from the beginning to the end. He never missed a thing that was going on around him. He played bridge like a fiend and always won. He remembered any card that was played.

Bill was great with Wanda's four boys. They had a love of fishing in common. They loved and respected him. If Bill Carr said something, that's the way it was. But he was…well; sometimes you'd just like to kick him! And why was that? Because he could tease. He loved to tease. For him, that was part of the love. If he didn't tease you he didn't care about you. He gave people a hard time, but they knew it was because he loved them.

Wanda's boy Lane mowed our yard sometimes. One time he needed gas to fill the mower. Bill told him it was in a red gas can in the shed. So Lane went down and grabbed a red can that he thought was gas and filled the mower, but it was kerosene. So, he told Bill and Bill asked, "What does it say on the side of the can?"

Lane answered, "Kerosene."

Bill said, "Didn't you read it?"

Lane said, "No. I just saw it was in a red can."

Bill made him dump it out of the mower, clean it out and put the gas in it. I always thought if he hadn't made him clean it out and do all that work, it would have gone right over Lane's head. He was a teenager. I think a lot of people might just have gotten mad at Lane or sent him home and that would have been it, but Bill was a teacher.

Bill really liked youngsters. Bill's oldest grandson, whom we called Billy, spent a week during his summer vacations with us soon after we moved from Milwaukie. I have two specific memories of these summers. The first was when Billy told me that I was a "good cooker." The second was when Billy was stung by a yellow jacket. I treated it economically with a mixture of baking soda and water. Bill's two other grandsons, and granddaughter, also visited us during briefer trips with their parents.

There was a young fellow staying with people across the street from us. This kid had a troubled background and Bill got to know him. They had something in common and that was Jazz music. Bill loved Jazz and so did this kid. At Bill's funeral this kid came up and handed me a folded piece of paper. He had written a poem to God about Bill. I can't remember much of it except the end where he said to God: "You've got a good one, this time."

Bill had just come home from work. Wanda and I were on the phone, talking city business. Wanda's oldest son, Mark, came hurrying in to Wanda's office and said, "Come right now! Bill Carr's in trouble!" We were still on the phone and Wanda said to me, "Charline, something is wrong with Bill."

I asked, "Where is he?"

Wanda answered, "On my front porch!"

Mark came and got me and drove straight up across the field...in his car. At that time there were no fences and Wanda lived just across the field from us on Columbia Avenue. I could look right up into Wanda's back door. When I got up there I found Bill lying on the ground. Lane was holding him with his head and shoulders in Lane's lap. I went over to him and the emergency siren was going on and on and on. Chuck

Harris, a volunteer firefighter, (and now our Fire Chief) showed up with his wife, who was very pregnant at the time, with their daughter Johanna. She was a volunteer firefighter, also, and was working with Chuck giving Bill CPR. I remember standing over him, horror struck.

Bill looked up and said, "Honey, honey…" That was all he said to me.

And then he said, "Don't let me go Chuck."

Chuck said, "I won't if I can help it, Bill."

But with such a massive heart attack he was DOA at the hospital. Wanda drove me in her car behind the ambulance. But I knew he was gone before we even got there. Bill had had a prior heart attack and was under a doctor's care with medication. I talked to his doctor later and asked him if there were anything that could have been done had he gotten to the hospital sooner. He said no. The only thing that could have saved him would have been if he had been in the hospital when the attack occurred and there had been another heart ready for a transplant. And of course, that couldn't happen. That was 1980. They may be able to do other things these days, but nothing could have saved him then. He is with us every day when we drive down William R. Carr Avenue. What a beautiful way to honor him. Bill was only 57 years old. I was 41, and exactly two weeks earlier, had won the primary election for Benton County Commissioner. He used to give Mary Wright a "bad" time, but gently. He'd say, "Oh Mary, you don't know what you're talking about."

She'd say, "Yes I do!" They'd go back and forth. She was with the group of people at my house after the funeral and my mother and stepfather were there, of course. My mother saw Mary standing in a doorway, crying. Mary spoke to her and said how she would miss Bill so much. And my Mother said, "But he always gave you such a hard time, Mary," in a kind of joking way.

Mary answered, "Well, I know, but I always knew he loved me." And he did. He loved people. He did a lot of work for the people and for the city. And as Mary said later, he was a lot of fun.

His funeral was held in the Prince of Peace Mennonite Church in Adair Village, and it was overflowing with attendees. Jim Ableman was on our council then. Jim and his wife Mo, and Bill and I were really close. Well, ALL of us were close. All of us socialized and worked well together. Jim was in such bad shape at the funeral, so overcome he had to be helped out of the building by two friends. Bill's death was a hard blow to many of us.

Bill Carr's Infamous Recipes

Uncle Willie's Chili

1½ medium onions chopped
1 medium green pepper chopped
1 large celery rib chopped
1 clove garlic minced
3 TBS Wesson oil
3 lbs ground round
1 lb ground fresh pork
1 lb sweet Italian sausage
6 TBS mild chili powder
1 TBS ground cumin
2 tsp garlic salt
1 small can chopped green chilies
salt & pepper to taste
1 can beer
1¼ cups bottled water
1 large can diced tomatoes
1 – 8 oz can tomato sauce
1 – 6 oz can tomato paste
1 bay leaf
1 can Swanson Beef Broth

To stock pot or large deep fryer, add a bit of Wesson oil and cook sausage, ground beef and pork until browned. Make sure all meats are cooked through.

Add chopped vegetables and cook until vegetables are transparent. Add all other ingredients.
Simmer, covered on low heat for about 3 hours, stirring often. Add beef broth gradually toward end of cooking time.

Remove bay leaf. Serve with saltine crackers and cold milk.

Optional:
Cook 1 lb of pinto beans separately. Add beans to cooking pot if desired.

Bill Carr's Famous Louisiana Gumbo

2 – 3 lbs chicken thighs
½ lb bacon
1 – 1 ½ lbs diced ham
1 lb sweet Italian sausage
2 lbs medium shrimp
2 lbs crab meat
2 medium yellow onions diced
4 stalks celery diced
½ green bell pepper chopped
¼ cup parsley chopped
6 garlic cloves minced
1 large can diced tomatoes
salt, pepper & ground thyme to taste
dash of ground red cayenne pepper
2 -3 bay leaves
1 -2 cups long grain white rice
1 can okra

In a large soup pot, place 2-3 lbs of chicken thighs and cover with 8–10 cups of water. Cook on low heat for about 1 hour until chicken is tender. Remove chicken from pot and place on plate to cool.

While chicken cooks, fry ½ lb bacon in very large skillet. Remove bacon, cool it, then crumble and set aside. Add 1-1 ½ lbs diced ham to bacon grease in skillet. Also add 1 lb sweet Italian sausage, 2 diced medium onions, 4 diced celery stalks, ½ chopped green pepper, ¼ cup chopped parsley and 6 cloves minced garlic. Cook all together in skillet until the sausage is done through.

Add this mixture to the chicken broth in the soup pot. Heat all together until hot, then add 1 large can chopped tomatoes, salt, pepper, and ground thyme to taste. Add a dash of red pepper and 2-3 bay leaves.
Remove skin and bones from cooled chicken thighs and return the meat to the pot. Simmer all together slowly about 1 hour. Add 2 lbs cleaned, deveined medium shrimp and about 2 lbs crabmeat. Add crumbled bacon to the pot and heat thoroughly.

In a separate pan boil water and cook desired amount of rice. Heat canned okra in a small saucepan. Remove bay leaves from gumbo.

Serve Gumbo in bowls over cooked rice. Add okra for those who want it. Serve with hot, crusty, buttered French bread.

Robert (Bob) L. King
1933–2014

Robert (Bob) L. King of Adair Village left this earth and was suddenly and unexpectedly taken to his home in Heaven at 6:45 Thanksgiving morning, Nov. 27, 2014. His place of departure was Good Samaritan Regional Medical Center in Corvallis.

He was born to Bertie Irene (Holmes) King and Hubert B. King on Oct. 17, 1933, at home in Alton, Missouri, the first child of four. The family moved to Camas, Washington, shortly before Bob's 10th birthday. Bob grew up in Camas, graduating from Camas High School. He earned an associate's degree from a community college in Vancouver, Washington. He served his country for two years in the U.S. Marine Corps, during the Korean War.

Bob worked for nearly 30 years as a mill manager for Crown Zellerbach Lumber Company, followed by his election to the Columbia County Board of Commissioners, for which he served one term. It was at this time that he met his future wife, Charline, while she was serving her second term as a Benton County commissioner. Bob and Charline worked together on a land use committee for the Association of Oregon Counties.

Following his term as a county commissioner, Bob was hired by the City of Turner for the position of city administrator, where he worked until his retirement nine years later. After Bob's retirement from Turner, he volunteered his expertise in Arby's Restaurant, Charline's business in Corvallis. He dedicated many hours, working as an oversight manager of the operations team until it was sold in April 1998.

As a resident of Adair Village, Bob then volunteered to work as city administrator for a six-month period following the retirement of longtime city administrator Wanda Tobiassen and before the hiring of the next administrator. Bob accepted no pay, choosing to receive recompense in water and sewer service for several months instead.

Of all Bob's jobs, his greatest joy was working for the Lord. He served as his church's treasurer and deacon for several years, until a major stroke in January 2003 forced him to discontinue. Until the day of Bob's departure for Heaven, he served as a prayer partner through his church, praying for those in and outside the church who had specific needs.

He often said he was sorry that he could no longer do more for his Lord. He read his Bible until it fell apart, and daily read his new Bible until the day of his death.

"Blessed in the sight of the Lord is the death of His saints." — *Psalm 116:15.*

Delores Pollard

Mount Jefferson can be seen on clear days from the pond.

Sheriff Jack Dolan
1935-1992

Gazette Times

Sheriff Jack Dolan

Sheriff Jack Dolan was Benton County Sheriff for 18 years. In 1974 the State Sheriff's Association (OSSA) named him Oregon Sheriff of the Year. He was in office longer than any other Benton County sheriff and had been in office for only a year when Bill and I moved here in 1973.

Jack was known all over the state because he was so future thinking and on top of things. He had a home along Soap Creek but he loved Adair Village. He also liked the fact that we were a new and struggling city, full of hope and enthusiasm. He was supportive and he helped us in ways that he really didn't have to. At that time we were meeting in the CISCO cafeteria. He would attend some of our council meetings, answer questions and find ways to help us. For instance, he came to our city council to help us set up the Neighborhood Watch.

One night we were having a council meeting and were parked in the big CISCO parking lot. The sheriff also parked there. He had his personal car, not the sheriff's car. It was night; our meetings were at 7:30. We were walking to the door and he looked around and there were a couple of guys siphoning gas out of his car! He hadn't even walked around the building yet. They ran and he ran after them. They realized he had seen them, but they didn't know he was the sheriff. He caught them and they were arrested.

We had several instances of gas siphoning in those days, but that was about the extent of the crime we had. Each time that happened, it was proven that those doing the crime were from outside the city. There seemed to be an attitude that because Adair was small, we couldn't do anything about it.

We didn't have police protection at all and Jack, of course, could not be here all the time, and neither could his deputies. But Jack told us how to set up traps for the criminals. We were able to catch some of them. Not physically, but we were able to get their license plate numbers, and we had some different ways we could turn this information over to the sheriff's department. That's what we did. It was truly a cooperative relationship with the sheriff's department during those times.

Adair really didn't need it's own police department because we had help from the Benton County Sheriff's Department as long as Jack was the sheriff. And we didn't have to pay for it. He just did it for free. He took us under his wing. We appreciated that.

The problem in short is that we don't have enough money to have a really effective police department right now. We want to have a police department in the future when the economy changes and we have more people here, the housing development is built, and we have more money. Right now the policies are all written. We have developed the foundation for a future police department.

I won the primary election for Benton County Commissioner in May of 1980. The general election in November arrived, and of course Bill wasn't there, but my parents were. They were retired and spent a lot of time with me because I was alone. Of course, I was nervous, nervous, nervous waiting for the returns. It was done differently then. We went to the polls and voted in person, which I prefer, instead of doing it by mail as we do now. You used to have to wait and wait for the returns to come in. So, we were sitting at the kitchen table, my parents and I, and the doorbell rang. There was Jack Dolan, the sheriff. It was in the morning around 10 o'clock and he said, "Well, it's Election Day and I know you must be nervous, so I just thought I would come and have a cup of coffee with you." So, in he comes and we all sat there and drank coffee and he waited with us.

Judi: That's really personable of Jack Dolan. Reaching out to you like that and being supportive.

Charline: Yes. We talked and he calmed me down. He said, "Charline, you are going to win. I know that. I just know that. You don't have to worry," and so on and so on. I was very close to him. He was a wonderful person. And he was right. I won that election.

An incident happened when I was living alone, and working in my first term as a Benton County Commissioner. I could not take care of this huge yard. Ray and Leona Savely, a couple who lived on the corner, knew about yard work and growing things, and they agreed to take care of the yard.

At this same time the people living in the duplex next door on the east side were kind of a shady group.

Neighbors living around here suspected it was a drug house because there were so many kids, teenagers and young people who would go into that house, be there for five minutes, and be out and gone. You would see this frequently, which made us suspect it was a drug house. We hoped Sheriff Dolan had his eye on it. Those people moved away from here and we were very glad.

After they moved, Leona was down here weeding in my vegetable garden. It was early summer and she came up to the house with some foliage in her hand and said, "Charline, do you know what this is?"

I looked at it and said the leaves reminded me a little bit of Shasta daises.

She said, "That's not what it is."

I asked, "Well, what is it?"

She said, "Marijuana."

"Where did you get it?"

She said, "In your garden, Charline!"

"My garden!" I said, "How did it *get there*?"

"I think I know." She explained that when she had been in the yard a while back, while the shady neighbors were still living there, she saw a guy come down to the fence and throw something over. She didn't think much about it because it was cherry season and there were cherry trees around and she figured he had some cherry pits in his hand and threw them over to get rid of them.

I thought, "What am I going to do with that? Here I am County Commissioner, oh, my gosh! I've got this growing in my garden?" Anyway, the next day I took it to work with me and went into Jack Dolan's office and said, "Jack, do you know what this is?"

He glanced at it and said "Well yeah, it's pot, why? Where'd you get it?"

And I said, "Well, um, it's in my garden."

He put his pencil down and said, "In your garden?"

I said yes, and explained how I thought it got there. He kept the plants and I didn't think too much more about it. But then every time we commissioners had a meeting with someone in the sheriff's office, usually Jack or the under sheriff, or a sergeant, Jack would come in and say, "Well, hi Charline, how is your garden doing now?"

Of course, nobody knew at all what he was referring to, except him and me.

Pastor Edward J. Miller
The Prince of Peace Mennonite Church

What is now Prince of Peace Community Church was originally the chapel for the Air Force station from 1958 to 1969. The church was a part of the property that had been conveyed to the Laborers Training Trust, a contractor's school. The Trade School did not want the church and sold it directly to a group of Mennonite people. Two other buildings were also up for sale: the NCO building and the bowling alley, which was privately purchased and became the Oakcraft furniture shop.

I was a member of The Prince of Peace Mennonite Church for 29 years, so I am very familiar with it and how it got started. The building had been vacated a number of years and there was a lot of damage to it, not so much vandalism, but weather damage. The Mennonites replaced broken windows, cleaned carpets and worked hard to do all the repairs before they held services there.

Ed Miller was the pastor at Prince of Peace Community Church for nine and a half years. He met with me when I was still the mayor of Adair Village and he said, "I think every city should have a newspaper." I told him there had been one, but Lorraine Ruff who produced it had moved away. He asked what the name should be, and I told him The Village Voice. He said, "I think that is a good name and I think the church should pick it up." I asked him what the cost would be and he told me about $150 for the first year. I said I would pay for the first year and I ended up writing a column. It came out once a month. It became quite a bit of work. We discovered a newsletter dated 1949, from the Adair Village Student Housing when Oregon State University used the old Camp hospital for veteran student housing after the war. It was called The Adair Spirit. I believe that having something that tells us what events are occurring is a universal human necessity.

A Note from Pastor Miller:

"I was called to Pastor the Prince of Peace Mennonite Church in 1979. A congregation of 30, including children, had purchased the Air Force station chapel on Arnold Avenue. During the next years the congregation grew to well over 200. Prince of Peace Church published a monthly newsletter. It was free and was hand delivered to every home in the village for many of those years.

Delores Pollard

Wayne Rudi carved the beautiful church sign, which is now gone.

The church also offered a preschool for the community for several years, meeting in our educational wing. This preschool was eventually co-opted by the Santiam Christian School next door to the church building, and for a time continued to use our classroom space.

We installed a large screen in the church sanctuary and featured educational and Christian movies for the community, including a series of Focus On the Family films, produced by Dr. James Dobson.

Numerous home bible study cells were held in the community and an annual, two week Vacation Bible School was conducted, including all grades from kindergarten through high school, even a class for adults. Prince of Peace Mennonite Church also packed the sanctuary by sponsoring a Change The World School of Prayer Seminar, attended by various denominations from the surrounding area. In order to accommodate increased attendance, plans were presented to enlarge the present facility. Those plans for expansion evolved into purchasing the plot of land on the northeast corner of Arnold Avenue and William R. Carr Avenue for the purpose of building an entirely new worship and educational facility. Unfortunately, Pastor Miller left sometime around 1990 and the new church was never built.

The current pastor, Kevin Ferguson, was called by the congregation to begin his ministry on the first Sunday of January 2016. A meet-and–greet gathering was held on February 14 in the fellowship room to welcome Pastor Ferguson and his family. This event was well attended by the Adair Village community.

Charline

I have a bank that was made in 1993 by Pastor Edward Jason Miller, from an original front plate that was used in the post offices at Camp Adair. It is a limited edition savings bank. The locking door is made of extremely tough bronze alloy. The bank itself is made of solid oak, with a slot in the top in which to drop coins. It is post office box number 216 from barracks number 42.

Judi

The post office boxes were assigned to each of the barracks. There were a number of post offices around the camp.

A Letter from Dan and Polly Callahan
Adair Village residents from 1974 to 1978

We came from Japan. We were both in the Navy. Polly was a nurse from Pennsylvania and I was a corpsman from Indiana. We left Japan in early 1974, got married, and drove to Oregon in April.

We had never been to Oregon, but decided that when we married we would move west, and Oregon sounded like a great place to start. We had a friend from the Navy - Dale Capriotti - who grew up in Oregon, and he moved back at the same time we did to attend OSU. We lived in a motel for a few days when we arrived in Corvallis and looked for a place to rent. We found Adair and rented half a duplex at 254 Azalea Drive.

Polly was hired at Good Sam Hospital right away and worked there the entire four years we stayed in Oregon. I continued in the navy reserves. I started at Oregon State University, in the summer of 1974, worked part time on campus for the Agriculture Department, and part time at Town and Country Veterinary Clinic on north 9th St. with Dr. Ross, Dr. Bilsland and Dr. Magden. We met good friends Bruce and Patty Koenig just down the street on Azalea Drive. Bruce and I bought a 1948 Chevy flatbed truck and an old 24" McCullough chainsaw and started a firewood business. We cut on BLM land and OSU land, but overall spent more money keeping the truck running than we made.

Dan Callahan

The back lots were wide, open fields when we lived here.

Polly's uncle, Bill Cavender, had purchased a couple of duplexes when the government decided to sell them a few years prior. Mr. Cavender needed around $1,800 for a down payment for someone to take over his VA loan at 170 Azalea Drive, just the amount we had in savings. So we took the plunge and became homeowners for the first time. When issues with water and street maintenance/snow removal etc. came up, the decision to incorporate became more important to us because we were homeowners. Bill and Charline Carr became our good friends. If you knew Bill, you still miss him like I do. Having the Carrs in Adair was a tremendous blessing because of their commitment to the community and their desire to make it a great place to live.

Dan Callahan

Councilmember Dan Callahan in front of his home in 1976.

I ran for city council when Adair incorporated and got to know the other council members as we worked on the immediate issues. Being an elected official at Adair was an amazing experience, pure simple democracy as it was designed to be. My specific first assignment was to find an accountant, Lou Ramus. We were also fortunate to find an attorney, Hank Dickerson, and to hire Wanda Tobiassen as our city clerk. These three unelected officials gave generously of their time, often for little or no pay, to help our fledgling city find its feet. Wanda lived in Adair with her family of four sons as I recall, and had a vested interest in our success. We were able to acquire the water system, much credit to Bill Carr and the council and others.

Dan Callahan

Dogs and kids loved to play at the pond.

We loved living in Adair - fresh country air and good neighbors. We were able to take walks past the old Officers' Club, across abandoned RR tracks to a pond where our dogs and kids could swim.

We also would drive to Camp Adair to the north and walk on the abandoned roads, enjoying the generous supply of black berries there. There was an Oregon State Wildlife station near there where the on-site ranger took in abandoned fawns that you could help bottle feed, and had quite a display of pheasants, including some exotic species that are marvelously colorful.

The homeowners association owned a strip of land between the duplexes on Azalea and the farmland to the north. It was only accessible from the adjoining property along Azalea, and we as homeowners were able to purchase some of this land. This gave us a place for a garden. There was nothing but farmland for as far north as you could see. But now it is all housing.

All the properties were built at the same time and all the hot water heaters were going out, causing damage to the oak parquet floors. Dale Capriotti and I started a small hot water installation project one summer. We made a deal with Wolfgang Dill to install water heaters in his 10 duplexes (20 units), and of course ours, making it 22. I wonder if any of those old state water heaters are still working today? We added a wood-burning stove to our side of the duplex at 170 Azalea Drive, and we still burn a lot of firewood where we live today in Ohio.

We rented the other side of our duplex to several different families: one came from Orange County, California and worked construction, but moved back because of the slow/laid back lifestyle in Oregon. One couple attended and worked at OSU, one family had their third baby in the duplex with the assistance of a midwife. One family had a Great Dane, one a St. Bernard, and one had pit bulls. We had three dogs, two from the pound and one a gift from our veterinary friend. There was never a shortage of dogs in Adair!

Dan Callahan

Driver's Training practice at E.E. Wilson Wildlife Area.

Some organization held driver-training exercises with orange cones set up on the roads in old Camp Adair. Our first son was born, and we continued to enjoy the community and added a stroller and a backpack to the walks. We were able to backpack, camp and cross country ski, usually on parts of the Pacific Crest Trail. We also went to the coast whenever possible. We loved the Oregon coast and had fires on the beaches in the evenings when camping in that area. Our CJ-5 jeep was great with the addition of sand tires, and we were able to drive the dunes down south of Waldport.

Polly's parents came for visits to go on the dunes and to go snow tubing at Mary's Peak. I had a four-man raft from navy days and we floated down the Willamette on occasion, usually starting around the Buena Vista Ferry. When Polly's family came to town we added another small survival raft and a couple of large inner tubes and floated all five brothers and sisters from Corvallis to Albany. We loved and still love Oregon, mountains, ocean/beach, desert, wildlife, and water falls.

On graduation in 1978 we sold the duplex. We asked for and were able to sell for much more than those properties had previously been valued. Since selling our home there in 1978 and moving to Ohio to pursue more education and eventually an Air Force career, we had not been back to Oregon for over 25 years. When we visited over Christmas about three years ago we were able to reunite with Charline and meet her husband, Bob King. Charline is still a driving force in local politics and still striving to make Adair a great place to live. It *is* a great place to live much more than most people realize, because of her dedication and hard work over the last 30-some years. Going back is always interesting. We noticed that somewhere over the last several years all the houses on Azalea Drive were moved closer to the street. Only a few of the old folks are still living there, but they remain friends and our memories of Adair Village will live with us as long as we live on this earth.

Delores Pollard

New play structure in the Kiddie Park since Dan and Polly left.

The Surrounding Area

Delores Pollard

The Rifle Range is not open to public use.

The Rifle Range

Northwest of Adair Village, the US Army Corps of Engineers Rifle Range is the only piece of the World War II Camp Adair still in use by the military. The Oregon National Guard firing range and open maneuver area at Camp Adair was renamed Camp Najaf in 2013. This name change memorialized a battle that took place in 2004 in Iraq, with heavy engagement of the Corvallis-based Bravo Company of Oregon's 2nd Battalion, 162nd Infantry Regiment. The Oregon Army National Guard and law enforcement agencies use the 527 acres of land and much conservation work has been done that benefits a number of rare or endangered species.

Delores Pollard

At the main gate of E.E. Wilson Wildlife Area on 99W.

Camp Adair Road

Honoring our servicemen at the E.E. Wilson Wildlife Area is a Veterans' Memorial Park. It has handicap access to a walk-through loop that honors the history of the four infantry divisions that trained at Camp Adair. See John Baker's *Camp Adair* for detailed information and join Gary Richard's group: I Remember Camp Adair at Facebook groups.

Delores Pollard

Memorial on Camp Adair Road.

The E.E.Wilson Wildlife Area is used for game bird breeding, controlled hunting, education and research. There is a photography blind, interpretive trail and viewing areas for public benefit at the show bird pens.

The preserve is one of the largest blocks of undisturbed wildlife habitat remaining in the Willamette Valley. About a half a mile down Camp Adair Road is a skeet shooting range and a recently added archery field.

Delores Pollard

New archery field harbors great rain protection.

Delores Pollard

The old Ivers' house was built in 1865.

Further east on Camp Adair Road are a couple of buildings, now the Dinnis Berry Farm, which were used by the veterinarians.

Delores Pollard

The Iver's barn at Dinnis Berry Farm.

The old barn was used for the guard dogs and the horses of the mounted patrol. Across the road is the old camp Ordinance Building.

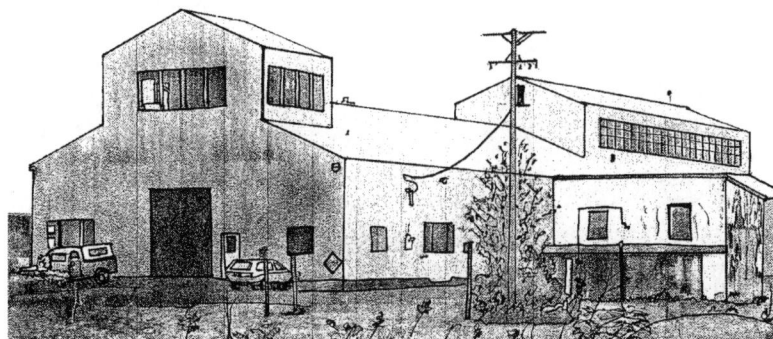

Delores Pollard

Oregon Fish and Wildlife utilizes the old Ordinance Building.

The PRC

The Pacific Region Compost (PRC) facility started in 1990 primarily to process wood products waste. PRC closed to the public in 2014, but composting still occurs there. Republic Services now operates the Pacific Region Compost Center and Coffin Butte, the nearby landfill.

Courtesy of PRC public website

Moving mountains of composted organic materials.

Republic Services brought in 20,000 tons of yard debris and food waste for composting in 2008. Now, it's closer to 120,000 tons a year. In roughly the same time period, cubic yards of compost created has jumped from 15,000 tons to about 100,000 tons. In the last five years, PRC has become the largest composting facility between Seattle and San Francisco. The compost Seal of Testing Assurance Program created by the United States Composting Council also approves its product.

Mid-valley residents can purchase compost at the recovery center at Coffin Butte Landfill, 29175 Coffin Butte Road. They can also drop off their yard debris there. It will be hauled to the Camp Adair Road facility for composting.

Delores Pollard

The Adair Park entrance on Arnold Avenue.

Adair Park

Adair Park was given to Benton County in 1972. It was a part of the recreational opportunities created for the Air Force station. At that time there were no parking lots or playgrounds, as there are now.

The building that housed the Officer's Club is now called the Benton County Park Clubhouse and is situated on the corner opposite the park entrance. It is outside the boundaries of the city.

Camp Adair historian Gary L. Richards said that one day while cresting the hill on 99W, he looked out and was astonished to see a jet plane flying so close to the ground that he could see the pilot. When in the area, the pilots try to fly exactly over the Officers Club...at high noon.

Adair Park is the largest, most developed park in the Benton County system. The park receives heavy use. Hiking trails are available, but sport poison oak.

Delores Pollard

The Gothic architecture, which is found in many historic Oregon churches, can be seen in the 125-year-old Palestine Memorial Church on Arnold Avenue in Adair Village. It is a Benton County restoration project.

Disk Golf Course

The County developed a disc golf course in 2001 in Adair Park, designed by the Willamette Disc Golf Club. Enthusiasts enjoy an incredible variety of holes. Some think it is definitely the best mid-Willamette Valley course for an advanced player. The course is frequently changing and evolving, making it even more fun for locals. See at Disc Golf Review: www.dgcoursereview.com.

Delores Pollard

Tee pad for hole #2 of 18 disk golf pads in Adair Park.

Benton County Radio Control Club

South of Adair Park is an area where Benton County Radio Control Club maintains an active radio-controlled aircraft aerodrome. The club was started in 1972 when Benton County received the park property from the federal government. This model airplane flying field was later named for William "Brian" Unwin, who was one of the founders of the club, along with James Trump from Trump Toy and Hobby in Corvallis. See Benton County R/C Aerodrome at www.rcgroups.com for the calendars of events and group discussions.

Delores Pollard

The aerodrome field along Arnold Avenue is a busy place.

Delores Pollard

The old Air Force gas station houses the model train club.

Model Engineers

Seven acres and one building, the former Air Force gas station, was deeded to Benton County in the early 1970's for model craft activities sponsored by the SW Division of Oregon Museum of Science and Industry. This is the home of the model train club and it is still active as of 2016. The Corvallis Society of Model Engineers (CSME) is a model railroad club that was founded in 1959. They have the second largest HO scale layout in Oregon. The layout recreates the feel of Oregon from the Oregon Coast, the Coastal Range, and the Willamette Valley to the Cascade Mountain Range. Station names are chosen from the cities of Oregon though no attempt to actually model these cities is made. The club railroad is called the Cascade Pacific.

The CSME open house is from 10 AM to 4 PM on Saturday and Sunday of the first and second weekend after Thanksgiving. This event has been held annually for more than thirty years. There is ample free parking and the layout is wheelchair accessible.

In the early 1950's the club was originally organized as The Corvallis Comets, a model airplane-flying club sponsored by the Corvallis Elks Club as a youth project. When the interest in model airplane flying waned, some visionary members approached the Elks about reorganizing to a model railroad club. Thus, the Corvallis Society of Model Engineers was born in 1959. When the Elks moved to a new building, the club lost its home and, in 1969, the CSME terminated its operations in the Elks Club. In 1971 the Adair Air Force gas station was declared surplus and Jack Culver, Julius Kilmer, Bill Freeman and Bob Lowry looked into acquiring the building to house the CSME. They incorporated the club as a non-profit organization and were successful in lobbying the county to acquire the building they are in now. The building came with seven surrounding acres. The agreement with the county allows them to use the property as long as the club exists. See: www.csme1959.org/index.html.

Delores Pollard

The old Air Force engineer's building houses Fish and Wildlife.

Corvallis South Willamette Watershed District

The Oregon Department of Fish and Wildlife (ODFW) acquired the huge army cantonment area of Camp Adair in 1948. The hospital area, on the south end, was returned to ODFW in 1951. The land was designated a wildlife preserve and named after E.E. Wilson, in 1950. Eddy Eldridge Wilson was a Corvallis native who served the ODFW for many years. He was considered a pioneer in game preservation and had devoted much of his time to fish and wildlife work.

The ODFW Regional Office at one time was in the Camp Adair Firehouse Number 5 building. They subsequently moved their offices to the Air Force

Engineer's building in 1979 and gave the old firehouse to Adair Village. The Adair pond is at the corner of Highway 99W and Ryals Lane. It has walkways, benches, picnic sites and fishing.

Delores Pollard

The Adair Pond is a pleasant picnic spot. There are often ducks or geese there, depending on the season.

When we were in school here in the 60's and my husband Eb's friends were in the service, we came to the commissary to buy things.

Judi

The pond was there then and they would swim at the "beach." It was a favourite recreational spot.

The Smokestack

A historic relic from Camp Adair, the smokestack was part of a heat generating plant for the hospital, which was built at the south end of the military cantonment. This solidly constructed brick chimney serves as a distinctive landmark. It is a consistent reference point on many of the old photographs and maps of the area. The smokestack is also a roost for the Vaux's Swifts on their annual flight migrating south to Central America. This swift is best known for its quick flight and dazzling

Delores Pollard

Smokestack left from Camp Adair.

aerial agility, perching only when nesting or roosting. In the fall evenings as they gather to begin migration, they swirl in large, black clouds, peel off in streams and pour down into the chimney. It is a fascinating sight.

Delores Pollard

McDonald Forest entry across from Adair Firehouse Number 5.

McDonald Forest

With an access on 99W, McDonald Forest is 7,229 acres of public land managed by OSU's College of Forestry. It supports research and educational opportunities and is managed for timber and other resources. Some of the projects date back to the early 1920's. Year-round recreational activities include running, hiking, mountain biking and horseback riding. There are some historic activities in the forest around Peavy Arboretum. Evidence can be found that the Civilian Conservation Corp (CCC) made use of the forest in the 1930's. Cronemiller Pond on the Section 36

Loop is a pleasant, quiet place to visit, except when the OSU log cutting and competitive activities are held there annually. The OSU Forestry students keep the trails in good condition and do regular litter control, among other things. The Arboretum houses the College of Forestry field office and staff. Arboretum maintenance is funded entirely by the College of Forestry with revenues derived from the sale of timber from the college forests. Peavy Arboretum is the home of the original Oregon State Forest Nursery and has an extensive collection of native and non-native trees and shrubs from the Pacific Northwest and other countries. Old growth forest still exists along Old Growth Trail and also along the Powder Trail. Douglas fir trees dominate the forest, but grand firs, western red cedars, big leaf maples and Oregon white oaks also are found.

Maps of the area are available. More information at the website: http://cf.forestry.oregonstate.edu/peavy-arboretum.

Geocaching

The old Camp Adair has over 70 geo-caching sites for those interested in this GPS (Global Position Satellite System) sport. By using satellite photographs and museum maps, historian Gary L. Richards of Suver located the central theater of Camp Adair. Before that, he located the Camp field house and the marker Have a Field Day, as well as Drink in the Past on Hospital Hill (Adair Village). The Village Smithy is the ruin of one of the blacksmith shops and Greater Love is one of the chapels. Another geocacher came to Gary with the Camp's northeast theater and the BOMARC missile site, as part of the Camp Adair Building Locating Exercise (CABLE). Mary Hardenbrook lived on a farm before the cantonment replaced it. She remembers as a child playing on a big erratic boulder, but so far it has not been geocached and remains obscured in poison oak and blackberry brambles. For more information see Camp Adair - a geocacher's guide at http:// campadair.webs.com.

Adair Village City Park

This city park includes a skateboard half-pipe petitioned by the city's youth in 2006, picnic tables, the barracks project and the Community Building.

Surrounding Adair Village are lands either in forestry, agriculture or wildlife refuge use. Along the east edge of Adair Village runs the Portland and Western Railroad (PNWR) whose offices are in Salem.

The Adair Rural Fire Protection District

Written from an interview: Fire Marshal Dennis (Denny) Haney with original volunteers Peggy Haney and Mary Hardenbrook, who has served as secretary of the ARFP for many years. Included is additional information supplied by Chuck and Fran Harris, Dick Green and Dave Campbell.

When DC-13 Adair Air Force station closed down in 1969, the property was released to the State of Oregon for redistribution. While the state decided what to do with the site, it contracted for fire protection for the housing area, because, although no one was living there, the state had assumed an outstanding mortgage debt on that property. But in June of 1971, fire protection was terminated. The Air Force property was located in a no man's land between the fire service district boundaries of Corvallis and Polk County. So, for a number of years there was nothing in the area in terms of fire protection. There were a couple of brush fires in the summer of 1972. That raised concern for some of us living in this area. A kid started a brush fire next to Tampico Road in the forest. Denny, a bunch of ladies and a whole bunch of kids put it out. The Forestry Department came and gave all the kids badges.

In 1972, the Chicano Indian Study Center of Oregon (CISCO) and the Oregon Southwest Washington Laborers Training Trust received property and began their programs at the former Air Force station. In 1973, the Boise Cascade wood products company took over the plywood mill, located in the old Camp Adair cantonment, which had been owned by Georgia Pacific since 1958. Many of the mill workers bought or rented houses in Adair Meadows, the Air Force housing that had been sold to civilian families and individuals.

On August 27, 1973 John Ankunding, representative for A. G. Proctor in the housing development called Adair Meadows then, was quoted in the *Gazette* Times. He said, "Adair Meadows does have fire protection... of a sort." He explained that he had fire hoses and couplings in his garage and "...several of the residents know about it and know how to use them!" To a firefighter, that is a scary scenario. The training is not something to take lightly.

On April 24, 1973, a *Gazette Times* article read: "Fire Station Could Bloom at Adair." The Benton County commissioners were very interested in fire protection because along with the start of these programs, more people were coming into the old Air Force station, and the surrounding rural areas were also growing. Jeanette Simerville, the first woman commissioner for Benton County, was involved, and again on May 22, the county commissioners talked about forming a fire station in the Adair rural district. It was a beginning, but nothing much official happened.

The Boise Cascade Mill, off old Camp Adair Road, was extremely interested in a fire department because it had frequent fires and once we were organized, we responded there regularly. Sometime in June of 1973, Irene Otjen, who was the office manager at Boise Cascade, approached the county commissioners about fire protection. Irene and her husband had owned a sawmill at Grand Ronde before they moved to Tampico Road. She was very aware of potential fire problems in this area. Mill manager Benny Christiansen and assistant manager Rod Brenneman were also involved right away but were never recognized for their efforts. The mill would receive an immediate financial savings once the district was established, because their fire insurance would be reduced. Irene Otjen was designated as the chairperson of the Fire District Organization Committee.

Irene persuaded some of the people in the rural area to be involved, along with Boise Cascade, Proctor's Adair Meadows, CISCO, and the Laborers Trust. Dick Green, from the rural Soap Creek area, submitted a petition for fire protection, as well. All these groups worked together and carried the initiative. We held planning meetings in the office at the plywood mill.

Elizabeth Harvey was involved at the beginning, too. She was the executive secretary for the Oregon State Soil Conservation Services in Salem. She lived on Harvey Lane and her husband built several of the houses along Tampico Road. Elizabeth was good at contacting neighbors, especially women, to get them to volunteer, mainly for daytime coverage. Irene and Elizabeth made a big difference. Irene was the spokesperson and Elizabeth kept the records and recorded the documents. Irene wasn't involved much after the district got off the ground. Elizabeth stayed involved.

The Benton County Commissioners organized a public meeting the evening of May 23, 1973. At that meeting Charlie Fox, Dick Foster, Danil Hancock, Terry Tollefson, and Don Mullett, who were rural residents, were chosen as members of an organizing committee. They started meeting at night, and my dear neighbor Irene invited me. I was not on the committee, but I went to all the meetings. I became the go-fer for the group. In the beginning, we didn't know anything about fire departments. So, I went to Monmouth, Corvallis and Albany on a regular basis and I got to know those three fire chiefs very well. I pulled together whatever information the group needed to know.

Soon things began to happen fast. Certainly the county wanted this done and the usual red tape must have been cut. One reason for that was the lack of objection from anyone to form a fire department. The fire district was formed by the end of the year. I don't think that could happen as quickly today. We have papers for June 4, 1973, from the State, which explains what it takes to form a fire district. Basically, it says to get your act together, get your paperwork in and do what needs to be done.

October 29, 1973, a description of the proposed fire district appeared in the newspaper, but it was rejected. The headline read: "Errors delay formation of fire department." I was part of the cause of that delay. Trying to write a legal description and get it accurate for 26 square miles of land in a short period of time was not an easy task. So, when we were on Arboretum Road and had to extend the district over to Soap Creek, I thought, "Why not just go straight across the hill?" But that went straight through MacDonald-Dunn Forest. My theory was if there is a fire somewhere in there, then we could address it. But that was not acceptable to the commissioners. The Benton County surveyor took over and re-wrote a proper description.

The process to form a legal fire district requires about three months and we had to have two public hearings to get input from the communities. Those meetings occurred on October 23 and November 13. No one came forward with questions about it, which sped things up. After the second meeting the commissioners authorized the formation of the fire district. It all started to gel around November 20, 1973. With Elizabeth Harvey on the committee, I have a sneaky suspicion that the paperwork was done right the first time, which was another reason it was expedited.

We became an official fire district on December 4, 1973. By the middle of the following January, there were 10 people applying for the board. Gene Abraham, Charlie Fox, Danil Hancock, Elizabeth Harvey, Guy (Mark) Holliday who was the chairman of the Adair Meadows Homeowners Association, Dr. Milo Merrill,

Alex Schaffner, Reuben Smith, Wayne Weigel, and Dennis Haney (me). Those were all fairly well known individuals around the area. Then we held the election for the directors of the board. Five of those members were elected: Gene Abraham, Elizabeth Harvey, Dr. Milo Merrill, Wayne Weigel and Charlie Fox. The board appointed me as the first fire chief.

The board had to develop a constitution and by-laws. There were legal documents that had to be completed and submitted to the special district's lawyer, not to mention that all the accounting had to be set up. At this point there was still no money for the whole project. A tax-base had to be developed from the map of the district. I had to look at the property values, and submit a budget, which I did. Then the cost was split up between the taxpayers. My first budget was for $24,747. We were a legal entity, but that was all. We had legal documents, lines on a map and a dedicated group of people, but no facilities, equipment or personnel. We started from scratch.

The previous May of 1973, the Laborers Training School had offered the use of the Air Force station fire department building, which was a part of their property, so long as they got free fire coverage from the fire district. The fire station hadn't been used in three years.

Paint was peeling from the walls. Flies and spider webs were everywhere. It was a mess on the inside. The community came together and helped do a major cleanup on the place and we moved in. Also, CISCO wanted to train some of their personnel as firefighters. We didn't see how that could happen. The problem was that there was no funding for staff to train them.

With all the contacts that I made, plenty of people responded with help. The Oregon Department of Forestry played a role. Jim Austin from the Dallas office was a prime source of information and a good resource for some equipment. He became a chief factor in the actualization of the department.

Denny: When we finally got to training, Chief Milligan in Monmouth said, "You must have a truck in there!"
I said, "We don't have a truck!"
He said, "I'll loan you a truck. You can have a truck."
So, he brought us down an ugly old GMC that barely ran, didn't have a pump tank or any fire gear on it but, by golly, we had a truck parked in there!

March 14, 1974 a *Gazette Times* article read: "New Adair Fire Department is seeking Firepersons." We advertised for members and took applications. There was a lot of interest at the start. It was a big turnout. We scheduled regular meetings to tell them what was going to happen and what steps we needed to take to get organized before we could begin with the initial training. It takes time to do all of that. We didn't even have a truck for a while.

Albany, also, really helped us through this whole start up. Initially, Albany Fire Department dispatched us on emergencies. We changed to Benton County when 9-1-1 was started. We bought an old 1948 Mack engine from Albany and a 1944 GMC tanker, with a 1,000-gallon water tank and pump on it. This old GMC was a military truck and it could go anywhere, but it had to have enough time to get there. If you pulled out on 99W going north up the hill, you were probably at the 25 to 30 mile an hour range. You might get up to 40 mph at the bottom of the hill but it was more like 15 when you got to the top. Mary Hardenbrook preferred to drive the GMC. Its ID in Albany had been T-8 (tanker) so we called it Tonka 8, because it was kind of a toy. I have to say the trucks were very slow. Their transmissions were old style and hard to shift. Little by little we have upgraded the equipment. Chuck Harris and Dave Campbell spent a lot of time building apparatus. Early on, they built a little attack engine out of another military rig.

Delores Pollard

The Fire station in Adair in 2004 before remodeling.

The County Emergency Services Director Jim Blodgett and Sheriff Jack Dolan, who lived up Soap Creek, helped us to get hand-off military equipment. They gave us two military trucks, both two and a half ton, all-wheel drive, GM, Korean War vintage. These trucks were converted into tankers.

One of the big selling points for creating the fire district had been the concern of high fire insurance rates. The Insurance Services Organization (ISO) is the company that sets the fire insurance rates and reduces rates if a fire department meets certain standard requirements. To pass the ISO test we had to pump 200 gallons of water a minute for 20 minutes, uninterrupted, which meant we had to have 4,000 gallons of water available to pump for the test. So we had 500 gallons on two engines and 3,000 gallons on GM tankers. We designed a manifold system where we stretched out a hose with special valves on it and trucks could pull in and hook up and pump. Then others could pull in and hook up and pump so we could pump that 4,000 gallons. We worked pretty hard on that and accomplished it in less than a year.

Delores Pollard

New hydrant at Carmen Place.

We achieved a Class 8 rating throughout most of the district. People never thought we would be able to meet those standards but we did! The classification runs from 0 to 10. An 8 saved about 50% on fire insurance premiums. Adair Meadows received a better rating because they had the water system with the fire hydrants. It took awhile to get the system in shape and get the hydrants fixed, but they received an 8 rating right away.

There was a schoolteacher in Adair Meadows who volunteered, along with her husband. Their initiation was a field fire. She came back from that and was just totally black! She was covered in ash and dirt! And loved it!

According to these papers the first training was April 24, 1974. We relied on firefighters from all the departments around us to come in and do training because they were experienced people who knew what they were doing. Don Milligan was here for the second and third classes. He was the Monmouth fire chief. Gene Wright and Stan Martin were from the Albany Fire Department. Jim Lewis was from the Corvallis Fire Department and Dan Wilkerson from the Lebanon Fire Department. These were the original instructors. They were all characters, but were excellent trainers.

These trainers were a really neat group, and they knew that we knew nothing! So, they came in full of stories that had strong educational value and a lot of safety training. "This is how you do it and you do it like this because you do not want to get hurt!" They taught us a lot. It was excellent training on the basics of what makes a fire burn, which is the first thing you try to teach people. They taught us the important information such as the chemistry of fire, fire behavior, portable extinguishers, basic pump operation, fire stream ventilation and structural fire attack. Those were the initial classes. And then to add to it, we watched *Emergency* on TV. Those were excellent fires.

Early live structure fire training began at a former migrant labor housing called Eola Village, near Amity, Oregon. Fire fighters from many entities trained on about eight buildings. Here we had our initial chance to enter a burning building using teamwork. This was a very meaningful training. It taught us the importance of working together safely, understanding just what was expected of our teams and the expertise of looking out for our teammates.

One of the memorable training fires, of many, was the block long refrigeration building for old Camp Adair. Besides us, there were crews from Albany, Corvallis, Lebanon and other places, who brought ladder trucks, fire engines, and water tenders. The walls on the building were two or three feet thick and full of sawdust, bees and honey! It took about one and half day to burn that building and we learned a lot!

Now, it takes almost three years to get through a training cycle because there are so many subjects. In the beginning and even today, a high priority is to take care of ourselves if we get hurt. An initial part of our training was to get everybody certified in First Aid. Chuck Harris was working at Evans Products at Lewisburg as an engineer and was one of the first volunteers. He grew more interested in the medical part of the whole thing, training to be an EMT (Emergency Medical Technician). More volunteers wanted that training. We wanted to be more than just a fire department. We wanted to offer medical response. So we took first aid courses, at our own expense, at Linn Benton Community College, for EMT Basic and Intermediate certifications. This was on top of our training events involving live fire training, vehicle rescue, and hazardous materials, and many of us were holding down full time jobs.

Then, since we were trained in it anyway, we wondered why we couldn't provide first aid to the public, too? It wasn't automatic. We had to have two public meetings before we got the proper authorization. We were soon able to increase our responsibility to provide public medical response.

Initially, we ended up with four trained EMT firefighters: Chuck and Fran Harris, Martha Campbell and Marty North. More soon followed. Other volunteers were trained as First Responders, which was a certification level between first aid and EMT training.

Eventually we gave trainings to the public in CPR and Emergency First Aid.

That first group of firefighter volunteers were all HP workers, college profs, schoolteachers, people that were in tune with happenings along the way. They were a very interesting group of people. We needed people with common sense. Mary Hardenbrook is an example of that. She was raised on a farm, had driven farm machinery, knew trucks, and had lived in this district since dirt was created. We would give her a problem to solve, for instance, to get a truck from here to there, or to get this pump started, and she already knew how to do it without any extra training. These farmer's daughters already had "know how." I'll take a farm person, anytime. When you ask for a bunch of volunteers and you say, "Come out for a meeting. Let's get this thing going!" you end up, of course, with a broad cross section of people.

The Albany Fire Department was our first permanent dispatch center. We were designated as station (area) 400. When 9-1-1 was implemented, Benton County became our dispatch center. Since that time, our station's apparatus and personnel have been identified with the prefix 1400. Eventually, a Mutual Aid-Mutual Response system of cooperation was developed where neighboring fire departments now assist each other to cover all calls for help.

On May 25, 1982, Jack Dolan deeded land for a fire department sub-station on upper Soap Creek Road. We built that station in 1984. That station extends the best rural fire insurance rating to the end of that part of our district.

There was a type of activity at fire departments called mustering. I don't think it happens much anymore. The departments would get together and practice old-fashioned firefighting techniques in timed competitions. They would pass buckets of water to a tank, pull hose on antique hose carts and use antique fire trucks to demonstrate pumping techniques.

We had quite a mustering team, both men and women. That training improved physical abilities and teamwork skills, which were reflected in the way the firefighters performed in an emergency. Mustering was a sideline, but it was important. It whipped the volunteers into shape because it was a lot of lifting and pulling and running, and there was plenty of moaning and groaning going on, too.

Our mustering team made history because in that day there weren't many women involved. The question was, "Do you take women?" We had to. If we were going to have any response we better have women! That is how the Adair Equal Rights Volunteer Fire Department was started and became a great success.

ADAIR VOLUNTEERS
THE
EQUAL RIGHTS
FIRE DEPARTMENT

The Commuter, LBCC

Some of the volunteers printed up a big sign, which they used for identifying themselves in the muster competitions. We went down to California and competed, and people came from other parts of Oregon and Washington to muster. We became well known around the area. It was really quite a big deal. People were serious about it. Our department held some records for a long time because of the skills and abilities of our firefighters.

In the rural communities, volunteering was a family affair. Everyone volunteered together, husbands and wives, and the children, when they were old enough. The older children helped with childcare while the older members attended classes and drills. That is the way it was when the department first began, and it is still going on now. Whole families went out together: The Hardenbrooks, Haneys, Denisons, Schaffners, Sarros,

Harris' and Campbells all went out together. That's pretty important. It brought the awareness of safety to a very high standard.

The Campbells and Harris' purchased this antique fire truck, and with the Haneys, spent hundreds of hours on its restoration.

Creating the fire district was a huge development, especially when we started from nothing. Once the department got started, it just went on and on from there. It is a going thing! But it is really, really hard to get personnel these days. Volunteer fire departments do not have the luxury of staff on hand to ready the equipment for the next alarm. Department engineer and captain, Dick Green, developed the first in-house equipment check system, called a 10-8 Check Sheet to inventory and repair equipment each time it is used for a call and returned to the station. This check sheet is used by almost all volunteer fire departments in Oregon today.

The size of the district has stayed about the same, but the population in the rural area has probably doubled. In the beginning people were much more aware of the need for protection than they are now. With service available, people get used to having it and take it for granted. The difficulty finding volunteers is a problem being experienced everywhere.

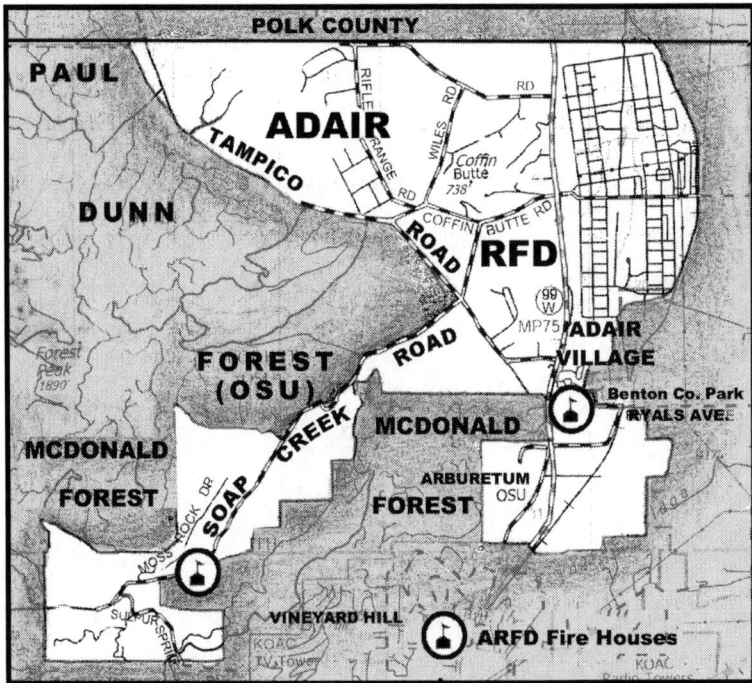

Modified from a 1974 State of Oregon Forestry Map. Delores Pollard

Denny: We moved here in 1968. I was always concerned about fires in the area. I'd been on the North Bend Department for a few months way back when I'd gotten out of high school, so I knew a little bit about fighting fires. I'd seen some fires in the past. So it always bothered me that we had the woods and the brush and all that here. We'd leave home and come back and say, "Well, the house is still here!"

I'm sure those kinds of conversations were occurring also with Irene. Irene is an interesting lady in that she was a gung-ho, get things done kind of person. As the office manager for Boise Cascade, she pretty much ran the mill. It seemed like the initial planning for a rural department started around our dining room table. Irene spent a lot of time at our house. She expressed concern about fires and asked, "What does it take to start a fire department?" Well, we found out!

The fire department isn't the Adair Village fire department, and it bugs us old timers in particular when the newspaper calls it the Adair Village Fire Department, which it is not. It just happens that the initial fire station was built by the Air Force on property that later became Adair Village. We are commonly known as the Adair Rural Search and Rescue but the legal name is Adair Rural Fire Protection District. That gives people a misconception about what it really is. Very often the people out in the rural areas think the city is going to come out and protect them. It makes it harder to get volunteers from the rural area, even though there is a good amount of people to tap into. It is a rural fire protection district. If we were to change the name again to clarify that, it would probably be The North West Benton County Rural Fire Protection District. But Adair Rural Fire Protection District says more about our roots.

Volunteers

Charline: Every time the *Smokescreen* newsletter comes out from the fire department they are asking for more people to get involved. Apparently they are not as successful today as they had been in years past getting people to volunteer.

Mary: Chuck's article is always asking for more volunteers. The newsletter is built around that message. I think that article hasn't changed for four or five years now. But we have a core group of really nice people, very good ones. We maintain anywhere from 12 to 15 firefighters.

I've always been really proud of Chuck and Denny. Here's Chuck, who gets involved and becomes inspector and just keeps going on with it. And Denny accepts every challenge that comes up with it.

Delores Pollard

The charming old mailbox.

Denny: We had "sleepers" at the fire department for quite a long time in the back room. Part of the advantage was having someone there. In the traditional old firehouses you think about pool tables and beer drinking, all the carousing and stuff but from the get go that was never, never, never, part of this department. We were volunteers dedicated to doing the job and we were serious about it. But when you get young college guys in there, sometimes things go on that you don't want to have happen. You don't want people wandering in when it's happening. So, that was a tough thing to try to police. We finally backed it off. Supervision was a tough thing. We had enough trouble watching our own kids let alone a bunch of college kids who ought to know better.

Adair Rural Auxiliary

Denny: One unofficial thing we started was an auxiliary for the department, when there was an emergency. We needed somebody to get drinks and food and things like that. Traditionally, it is the firefighters' wives, but Mary was on the fire department, so her husband became our auxiliary. We'd say, "Call Glenn!"

Mary: He didn't want to be part of the fire department but, even though I couldn't talk him into joining, he would go with me. He didn't have a problem with me going, which I thought was nice.

Denny: He was sure a valued member!

Mary: On one of his birthdays we threw him a party and I found a t-shirt for him that said the Women's Auxiliary. He didn't like that a bit. It was supposed to be a joke. He took it into the T-shirt shop and had it blanked out and had Men's Auxiliary written on it. And of course, we never let him forget that, either!

Dump Fires

Mary: Sometimes we'd get the dump burning.

Denny: It is our only industrial complex. Back when we first started the fire department, they were very supportive of it because the dump caught on fire on a regular basis. There was industrial dumping and as soon as the fall rains hit they started having fires.

Mary: Rain reacts with certain metals. Wah Chang was dumping refuse that was exotic metals. If something heated up and then the water hit it, you'd have a big fire.

Denny: We had all sorts of fires. I got very disgusted one time. Reporters wanted to make some kind of drama.

Mary: Yes, they wanted to know who's to blame.

Denny: They were very persistent. I finally told this one reporter that, "We've got a landfill fire. The major things thrown away in landfills are baby diapers. We had a huge fire in burning baby diapers. What more can I tell you?" I don't remember him ever coming back.

Do you remember the days when we used flashcubes on our cameras? Those little square blue things? When you triggered it, it would flash. Do you know what was in the flashcube? Zirconium. Those fine filings were made over at Wah Chang. It was their garbage. When you hit that stuff, there was a little strike and it went off.

Mary: Do you remember when Wah Chang did the demonstration for us? They put the little pile of shavings on the grass next to the Blockhouse. We moved clear over on the other side of the parking lot and the guy was out there with his full protective suit on. He lit that little bitty bag off and we felt the heat clear over there.

Denny: I've since had to do several fires there at their facility. The refuse from there would start several fires a year. You had to be careful. Not get too close. You definitely didn't want to drive a truck on it.

Mary: We had a fire once early in the morning, about four AM. We had this neat little truck...

Peggy: Mary's truck. The Tonka 8.

Mary: I wish we still had it. It was a great little truck. It didn't have any doors. It would climb up anything.

Denny: It was a 1944 GMC, deuce and a half military truck.

Mary: We got up to the dump and Denny told me to take the truck somewhere else. Well, the truck is high so the headlights were not shining on the level ground where I was parked. I'd never been up to the dump before and lo and behold they have a gol'durn pit! I'm making a nice big turn and all of a sudden I'm hanging on the edge of the pit. The front wheels are sunk into that soft stuff and that is what stopped it. The tailboard of the truck was way up in the air. The poor kid on the back, it was a wonder she didn't break a leg jumping off. The guy in the pulpit in the front had to climb up over the hood. He saw it coming, brought his arm up and stopped me.

Denny: Kerry Goonan. He got out of there quick.

Mary: We stayed there for an hour.

Delores: How deep was it?

Denny: About 30 feet.

Mary: I said to Denny, "Well, I think I can probably drive this down." He said, "No, I don't think you better try that." If I'd tried it I probably would have been dead.

Mary: Old Denny, you couldn't faze him, he was just as calm as could be, and said, "I don't think we better do that!" We ended up pulling the thing off the edge. Couldn't even fight the fire till we got that stupid truck hauled off the edge.

Denny: Luckily we had a truck with a winch and pulled her out. I said, "Hold your foot on the brake now, Mary."

Mary: Oh, Lordy, I was already jammed down so hard down on that brake!

Peggy: You had a charley horse for days!

Mary: I went home and got ready for work and said to my husband, "I've got to go see this." We drove up there and I looked over the edge and, I'm not kidding, I know what flashbacks are! The rest of the day I'd be typing along when all of a sudden there I was- hanging over that edge! Holy cow. It was funny, really. We got a charge out of it, after it was over, I mean.

Adair Rural Fire Protection District
First Roster (July 1, 1974)
Chief Dennis Haney

Company 1
Captain Chuck Harris
Lieutenant Phil Sarro

Company 2
Captain Steve Beckham
Lieutenant Allen Hadley
Lieutenant Dave Standley

Company 3
Captain Dick Green
Lieutenant Bill Denison

Fire Fighters:
Abraham, Eugene
Beckham, Steve
Denison, Tom
Denison, Bill
Green, Dick
Hadley, Allen
Hancock, Danil
Haney, Dennis
Haney, Peg
Hardenbrook, Mary
Harris, Chuck
Harris, Fran
Harvey, Elizabeth
North, Jon
Sarro, Pat
Sarro, Phil
Schaffner, Alex
Schaffner, Elizabeth
Shearmore, Steve
Standley, Dave
Terry, Bud
Tucker, Jim
Warren, Ann

Part 5:
Businesses in
Adair Village

Delores Pollard

Painting the Firehouse white in 2004. It used to be blue-gray.

Adair Village Food Mart

6002 NE William R Carr Ave.
Adair Village, OR 97330
541-745-2014

A young couple from Philomath, Ed and Coleen Lossett, opened the first store in the east section of the old Camp Adair Firehouse Number 5. Later on, the west end of the building was leased as a consignment store and was run by women from the local Prince of Peace Mennonite Church. Another local couple, Malcolm and Debbie Rose, owned the store for a while.

Bill and Kay Hanna opened the AV Pub and Market in 1989 and operated it for 17 years. Their son, Charlie, ran the Pub until a fire broke out after closing one night, which severely damaged the building.

Charline

The first store opened in May 1980. I was so glad to see a little store open there in that space. Before then you had to go to Lewisburg if you needed milk or something like that. It became the store farthest north along 99W.

Wanda

Ken Udahl, who worked for Fish and Wildlife in the old firehouse, wanted additional streetlights turned on there. He wanted one close to the building and paid for the lighting. He later sold the building and property to Adair Village. The city owns the land between 99W and the south end of William R. Carr. We lease the buildings.

Gerald Patrick Jacobson, from the research paper he donated to the city.

The Firehouse Number 5 building in 1977. No front doors!

After the Pub closed, the city was not sure what to do with the building. Many wanted to renovate it, especially some folks in the fire department. The city council made the decision to renovate the building. Candice Dinnis was hired as the Project Manager and she did a great job for us. The city's fire insurance, $114,000, covered the majority of the renovation cost.

Delores Pollard

AV Food Mart, 2015, before Farm Food came with brown paint.

When the workers pulled up the old carpet, the beautiful 1940 Douglas fir flooring was revealed. Candice hired professional restorers to come in and save the old flooring. The building was empty for nearly two years until Ed and Lois Dasteur opened the Village Food Mart in June of 2008. They opened their restaurant and named it Firehouse Number 5. When the economic downturn halted the expected growth of Adair Village, the business closed in 2013.

Delores Pollard

The Firehouse Café was the first restaurant in Adair Village.

Charline

All businesses long for more population for enhancement of their sales. We look forward to the future development of the neighborhood in the urban growth boundary to the south for this. Hopefully that will happen soon.

A new convenience store opened immediately after the Dasteurs left. The Village Food Mart name remained, but the interior was painted and reorganized inside. The new owner, Paul Johal, owns several other convenience stores in the region. His brother-in-law, Nirmal Mahli and his family run it now, in 2016.

AV Food Mart serves Adair Village for convenience buying, dairy, snacks, wine, and an ATM. You can still see the big fire station doors on the east wall. The restaurant side of the building remained vacant until 2015.

Delores Pollard

Adair Village Food Mart in a wonderful spring rain of 2016.

Delores Pollard

Farm Food

Farmfoodrestautant.com

Jim Jones

Everyone was thrilled when Jim Jones opened his fine dining restaurant in Adair Village in July of 2015. Jim is currently in restaurant development with a new concept. He runs his restaurant featuring foods from farms big and small, paired with wines and beer. The new concept uses only chefs as staff members.

In the past Jim has received the Wine Enthusiast Award of Distinction from Wine Enthusiast Magazine and Wine Spectator magazine's Award of Excellence. He plans to do the same at Farm Food.

The restaurant takes no reservations in order to accommodate local patrons. They cannot accommodate groups larger than six people but are available for private parties.

Photo courtesy of Farm Food website.

The atmosphere inside Farm Food is friendly and relaxing.

Photo from Santiam Christian School

Santiam Christian School

Lance Villers, Superintendent
7220 NE Arnold Avenue
Adair Village, OR 97330
www.santiamchristian.org

Santiam Christian School (SCS) is a private Christian school in Adair Village. It opened in 1979, taking over some of the property that CISCO and the Sweathouse Lodge had vacated in 1977. The federal government awarded SCS a 30-year deed for $1, which expires in 2019. The people in Adair Village were delighted to have Santiam Christian School come into town. They are well respected by many, many people, which had not been the case with their predecessors.

Santiam Christian School was a breath of fresh air. Their reputation is good for the city.

> ## Mission Statement:
>
> The primary purpose of Santiam Christian School is to assist parents in the Christian training of their children by providing a Christ-centered academic environment that encourages the development of a Christian world-view emphasizing academic excellence, Christian character, responsible citizenship, and service to others.

The school has been accredited through the Northwest Accreditation Commission since 1993, and the Association of Christian Schools International. They are assigned to the West Valley League and emphasis is placed upon participation, with an extremely high percentage of students involved in at least one sport. The *Oregonian* newspaper has awarded Santiam Christian top 3A school in the state, for 10 out of 11 years.

Santiam Christian does not discriminate on the basis of race, color, national and ethnic origin in administration of its educational policies, admission policies, tuition assistance program, athletics, and other school-administered programs. Attendance for 2015 is around 610 students for the preschool through twelfth grade and there is a low student to teacher ratio. The peak attendance was 850 students in 2007-8, but when the economy took the dive, they lost about 250 students.

Santiam Christian partners with parents to fashion a Christian upbringing for their children. Professionally trained Christian teachers at all levels, quality curriculum and excellent facilities, combine to produce a total Christian education package. The requirements for high school graduation fulfill those of the Oregon State Department of Education. At Santiam Christian, a student must take a course of Bible study during each year in attendance. Along with the core curriculum, elective choices include classes such as art, business, drama, foreign language, music, shop, science labs, and computer labs. The school offers excellent academics and activities, from elementary to high school, and SC students perform well in the classroom, on the field, and in service to others and as they proceed into future learning opportunities. The classroom style is a traditional approach, where classroom discipline, modest dress, respect for authority, and a genuine desire to learn are characteristics that can be observed.

One of the nice things Santiam does, not only for Adair Village but also for Corvallis, Albany and the surrounding area, is the Service Day. Troops of strong boys and girls volunteer to help with projects in the neighborhood homes and yards. They can be seen digging holes, weeding, putting up fences, mowing, painting, and cleaning. The groups are well organized and all the students work with an enthusiasm that is uplifting.

The brick laying project is a fundraising program to help pay for part of the new building. People can buy a memorial brick to help pave the pathway between the new building and the gymnasium. If you would like to contribute to the building fund in this way please see the SC website. Bricks differ in size and price.

GO EAGLES!

One of the unique requirements offered at Santiam Christian School is a class called Character Education. A Bible verse is chosen as the theme of each year. The theme for 2015 used Proverbs 11:3 and "The integrity of the upright guides them."

Delores

Emails are sent out daily to the faculty to share and to talk about during the day. What comes across for me in this is the idea of feeding our minds with the living Bread of Life, tapping into spiritual awareness.

I know this works because I had a SCS student knock on my door the last day in September. He handed me a sandwich bag with a couple of grapes and some cracker crumbs in it. He said someone he knew threw it at a friend on a bike and he saw it land in my yard. He said he was telling me this so it would not be left there as litter. He was open and clear and wanted me to know what had happened. I really appreciated that.

I saw on the website that the character trait being studied that month was truthfulness. What a great kid! What a great school!

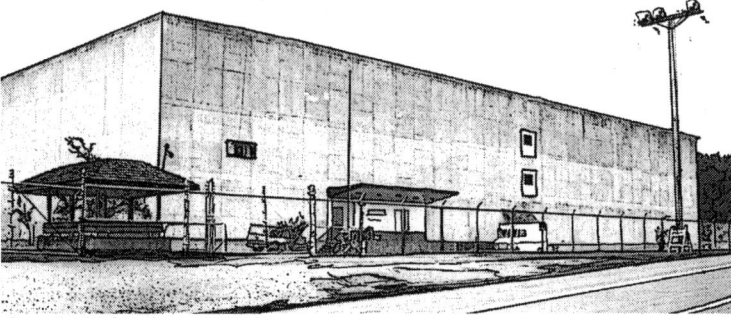
Gary L. Richards

Adair Commercial Center
J.F. Seely Building

Justus Seely
7170 NE Arnold Ave
Adair Village, OR *97330-9443*
541-740-8307

Adair Commercial Center (ACC) is housed in the J.F. Seely Building. Adair Village residents formerly knew this building as the Blockhouse. The building is named after the father of Justus S. Seely, who owns the building. Dr. Seely was a professor of Statistics at Oregon State University for 32 years. He was chairman of the Statistics Department for 11 years and later Associate Dean of the School of Science.

Justus Seely, from Willamette Valley Carpenters Union, purchased Adair Commercial Center in March of 2002. The Union had purchased the building in 1975, from the Oregon SW Washington Laborers Trust, who had received it with their federal property grant in 1972.

The two most prominent businesses housed in ACC are Design Tops Inc. and 4 Spirits Distillery. Design Tops Inc. was established in 1994 by Justus Seely and was formerly located on 99W in the Lewisburg area. Design Tops Inc. moved into ACC when Mr. Seely purchased the building.

Design Tops Inc. is a construction company specializing in home remodeling/renovation and floor coverings. The company sells and installs carpeting, vinyl flooring, cabinets, counter tops, as well as doing interior and exterior painting. Design Tops Inc. is also a licensed distributor of Empire and Cascade Windows. Design Tops Inc. employs four or five workers annually.

ACC has housed, and currently houses, other businesses as well, such as a small artisan woodshop. A large paint ball arena was staged on the upper floors, and rock bands use it for practice rooms. A well-known New York Times best selling author rents The War Room in the building, drawing on the military history of the building for inspiration. Corvallis Helicopter is also a past renter and stores helicopter parts and fuselage(s) used at the Corvallis Airport. Private individuals and organizations rent several areas for storage.

Caretaker Tim Hutchison maintains beautiful flowering plants on the grounds of the property.

Some residents of Adair rent the mini storage sheds as well as the RV and trailer storage spots on the property. For leasing information please contact Justus.

Delores Pollard

A huge gravel pile in 2015 nearly dwarfed the ACC building. Benton County has since moved their gravel storage site north to a piece of property on old Frontage Road. Thank you! But the neighborhood kids and their dogs sure miss the challenge of climbing it.

Delores Pollard

4 Spirits Distillery

Dawson Officer
6040 N.E. Marcus Harris Ave
Adair Village, Oregon 97330
503-999-7758
www.4spiritsdistillery.com

Dawson Officer opened his micro distillery business in 2010. He named it 4 Spirits Distillery to honor four Oregon National Guard comrades with the 2nd Battalion of the 162nd Infantry Regiment, who died in Iraq in 2004. Dawson wanted to create a dedication bottle for the four who did not return. He designed a logo and ran it by his fellow veterans and officials of the Oregon Military Department, including his former commander in Iraq. The design utilizes the "soldiers' cross" which is the soldier's gear stacked in a special way, with the helmet on top of the gun, the gun inside the boots and the dog tags hung on it.

They all agreed that it was a respectful tribute, not only for the four friends he lost, but also for all of America's fallen soldiers. The 4 Spirits Bourbon Whiskey comes in a distinctive moonshine bottle, a squat glass cylinder with a finger ring for easy hoisting. Attached by a short chain is a metal dog tag stamped with the silhouette of four GIs, which serves as the logo for the business.

The 4 Spirits Bourbon Whiskey, batched in 2012, won the Spirits International Platinum Prestige Award, which is the top award given at the 2013 World Spirits Competition. It also took the Silver Award at the SIPS (Spirits International Prestige) competition in San Francisco. His 4 Spirits Vodka took the Washington Cup's Silver Medal in 2014. The distillery produces vodka labeled Webfoot and Slap Tail, for Duck and Beaver fans. Following this inspiration additional lines are forthcoming: a Sundogger Vodka for the Washington Huskies, a Firecats Vodka for the Washington State Cougars, and a Buckin' Vodka for Boise State. As his expansion continues so will the line up of his uniquely designed brands.

Along with whiskey and vodka, Dawson also produces award winning flavored rum. He ages the rum in new American whiskey barrels, which gives it a wonderful whiskey-sweet taste. He currently makes four kinds of rum, including a Spiced Vanilla and Habanero Spice Rum. He holds a Gold Microliquer Award for spiced rum. He also recently released his 4 Spirits American whiskey, which is a four-year corn whiskey, the label being a well-known depiction of the Cavalry Scout.

Dawson started small but his product and his reach is growing. He is from the old school that believes in building his business carefully, without large loans and without going into debt to investors. He likes to think it is the right way but is finding it a slower and harder path. His dreams are big. He has one full time employee and three part-time workers, but does not yet take wages for himself. He has a wife who works and is very supportive of the business and the high ideals. It seems to be working because he has already expanded into six nearby states in the Pacific Northwest. People are getting the Fallen Soldier message that he is sending. There is not anyone with a mission like his and a story like his. It is tragic, but it is a good message.

Dawson donates at least 10 percent of the profits, generated from the dedication bottle of his 4 Spirits Bourbon Whiskey, to benefit veterans' services. He donates to combat veterans in Washington, Idaho, Wyoming and Montana in addition to Oregon. As a part of that tribute, Dawson created the 4 Spirits Veterans Scholarship Endowment Fund for Oregon State University, (OSU) in Corvallis to help pay for the education of military veterans. Is it surprising that this is the first Veterans' scholarship ever started at OSU? Dawson is the youngest person in OSU's history to start an endowment fund. This 4 Spirits Veteran Scholarship will try and fill the gaps that the GI Bill and other government-funded sources don't cover for our combat veterans. It's these gaps that force our veterans either to not apply for college or to have to drop out because of lack of funds. If you wish to contribute, contact: dawson@4spiritsdistillery.com.

Delores Pollard

Valley Catering At The Club House

Facility Rental and Party Planning Services
6097 NE Ebony Lane
Corvallis OR *97330-9492*
541-745-7455
valleycateringinc.com

For 22 years, Mary Bentley owned and operated the Valley Restaurant in downtown Corvallis. It opened in 1977 and was a popular local establishment that fulfilled many requests for catering services. As Corvallis grew, the need for catering weddings, social events and corporate events, such as meetings and conferences, increased. In 1998 Mary started her own business to handle the catering side of the restaurant. Valley Catering, Inc. opened in the Benton County Clubhouse, which was the Officer's Club when the Air Force occupied this area. Technically, Valley Catering is not part of Adair Village, because they are not within the city limits, but they have been here for 17 years. The building is rented from Benton County, but technically still belongs to the government. Mary had to apply for a concession permit from the National Park Service to operate her catering business on the property.

With remodeling and upgrades, the Clubhouse has become a first-class venue for fundraisers, weddings, retreats, small conferences and parties. Located just across the street from Adair Park, it embodies a peaceful atmosphere for special events and occasions. The Clubhouse dining room overlooks a beautiful garden patio setting and seats up to 135 guests. Using the patio, lounge, and dining room, 250 guests can be accommodated in the summer. There is plenty of parking on-site. The Adair Clubhouse is available for rental all year.

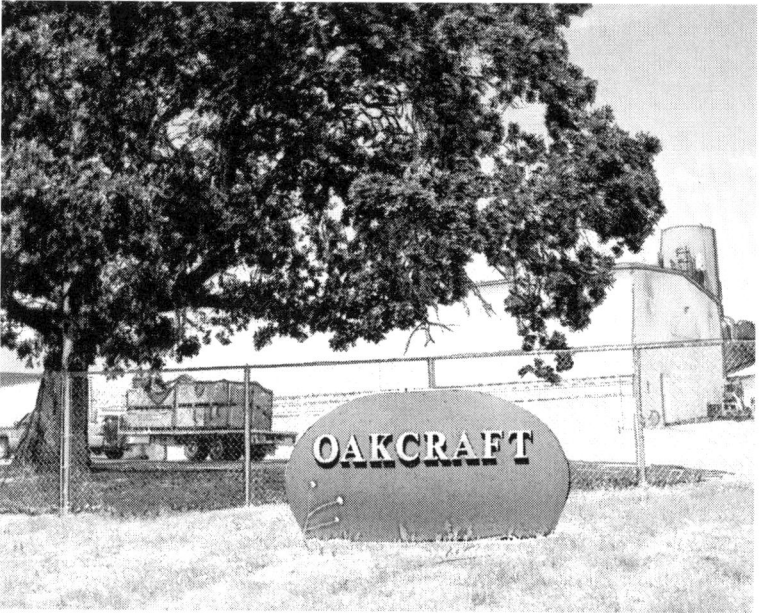

Delores Pollard

Oakcraft Manufacturing, Inc.

Brian Weekly
7269 NE Birch Lane
Corvallis, OR. 97330
oakcraftfurniture@gmail.com

After the CISCO property was deeded to the Laborers Trust in 1977; the Air Force bowling alley was sold to Alan Gibbs. Ted Cain leased it and together with a partner, Ed Seifker and his two sons, Ray and Paul, opened RCR Woodworking, Inc. in the building.

Ted was an elder in the Mennonite Church and a friend of Charline. He crafted the wooden swing that hangs on her front porch. He was also a member of the Adair Village City Council. In November of 1980, Charline resigned as mayor to take her first term as county commissioner in January 1981. The city council appointed Ted as the second mayor of Adair Village to fill out the last two months of Charline's term.

In the early 1980's, Brian Weekly was working for local furniture stores to help pay for college. In the warehouses he repaired damaged furniture and prepped items for delivery. One of the places he worked was Gibbs Furniture. The owner's nephew wanted to go into business making furniture and offered Brian a job doing the finishing work. Brian accepted and rented a workspace in North Albany. When the business folded, Brian decided he had enough experience to begin making his own furniture.

He already had the shop rented, so all he had to do was get a couple of saws and cut the parts. So he got busy and started making a few bookcases and taking them to the stores. Brian said he went out on the limb and decided he would do that for a while and go back to school later after he made some money. His dad asked him, "What are you going to do when the day comes that everybody has your furniture and nobody will buy anymore?"

He felt he had something to prove to his dad, "I'll show you that I can do this." So he worked night and day and every hour of the day that he was awake and that is how he did it. Brian said, "I worked for $3 an hour but I worked 20 hours a day. Every extra penny I put into machinery."

"Then around 1990, a furniture sales representative, Sue Jacobs, discovered my work and tracked me down. She became the best sales rep and friend, ever. She did me right. She put her heart and soul into it and expanded the business like no one else could. She just retired this September. My sister Becky also was here for a long time working with me."

Brian asked Ray Seifker to come and help him, so Ray is back in the building where he started with his dad and brother in 1979, although now it has been expanded to cover 24,000 square feet. Ray is the mastermind behind a lot of the process. In his machine shop he actually invents the machines they use to assemble the pieces. He makes everybody's job easier. He loves the challenge of figuring out how to create precision machines to solve problems. This helps make the process consistent, fast and fun. He is a really good woodworker; understanding exactly what is needed.

The old Air Force five-lane bowling alley is used as the finishing area. You can still see the triangle pin pattern that was painted on the oak floor at the end of the lanes, but the pin setting machines are gone. Brian remarked, "I always say you can't get any flatter than a bowling alley floor to make sure the angles are square when building your furniture."

Oakcraft makes a variety of furniture in oak and cherry including bookcases, office file cabinets, and platform beds with storage drawers and desks. The wood they use comes from 100% certified sustainable forests. The sawdust and scrap wood are ground up and sold to particleboard manufacturers. It doesn't go to waste.

For Brian, every piece he makes has to be something he would put in his own home. "That's how I have always done it. If it's not good enough for me, then it either gets torn apart or something else done with it, because the buyers are not going to have to fix my furniture when they get it."

That was the whole start of his furniture business. Brian was tired of fixing new furniture. It just didn't make sense to him that new furniture would come into the stores with the little taped edges peeling off. "We don't use any veneer tape here, it's all solid wood."

"I'm running a hundred miles an hour all day and am still always about three days behind and trying to catch up. Every once in a while I remind my dad about telling me I would run out of customers to buy my furniture, but I am so busy right now I can't build it fast enough. We moved out here to Adair Village in 1991. We are still here and I can't imagine moving again."

Delores Pollard

Sequoiadendron giganteum on Laurel Drive.

Delores Pollard

Sweet Taste Bakery & Coffee House

Don and Linda Hogan
6020 NE William R. Carr Avenue
Adair Village, OR 97330
541-207-3126
Sweet-Taste-Bakery.com

Before Sweet Taste Bakery arrived in town the spot they stand on now was a vacant hill owned by the city. The first establishment built on that hill was called Jamocha Jo's Java and Ice Cream and was built by

Kevin Higgins and his wife, Nancy. In 2006, they incorporated in Oregon and opened for business.

Kevin designed and built Jamocha Jo's from the ground up. He designed the building, inside and out, down to the parking lot layout. They were greeted with enthusiasm from the locals and the school students and staff. In the summers they held outdoor music concerts to bring even more customers and fun to the area of Adair Village. Kevin built a stage with professional lighting and sound system. The business was in operation from 2006 to 2012 when it closed.

Jamocha Jo's #2 had a short life in Adair Village. Lu An Carone ran it from early in 2014 until the middle of the summer. The building was sold to the city and it stood empty for a while.

Linda Hogan had been baking caramelized popcorn and cookies and selling her baked goods at holiday bazaars. People loved them and they sold well, so she began looking for a place to open up her own shop. Seven months later she showed up one day and took a look at the Jamocha Jo's building and fell in love with it. It had everything she needed. It was perfect for what she wanted. She approached the city council and brought along some baked goods for them to try. Another bakery business was also interested in renting, but the vote went to Linda. It was a good decision. With some new signage and equipment changes she opened on March 9 of 2015, much to the appreciation of Adair Village and the surrounding neighborhoods.

Linda made some caramelized popcorn for a Saturday 4 Spirits tasting event. It was made with Dawson's Spice Buttered Rum. Linda used rum flavoring and Dawson's products. The alcohol burned off, of course. It turned out well and everyone loved it. Her popcorn is delicious and sells so fast it is hard to keep on the shelves. Caramel Apple is the fall special. Butterscotch is the all time favorite. Since Sweet Taste is also a Coffee House, Linda wanted to try an experiment. She created Espresso Coffee Caramel popcorn. It was delicious but didn't go over well with the public.

There is a convenient drive up window, indoor seating for small group meetings, and free WIFI. An assortment of homemade treats that are baked fresh every day to go long with freshly ground coffee and specialty blends. Season favorites and day-of-the-week specials add even more variety. For breakfast anytime, select from burritos, or sandwiches on croissant or English muffin. Soups for cold weather lunches are available. Visit the website for weekly specials.

A word from the ghostwriter:

I met almost every Friday for three years

Delores with the Adair Diary women to write this story. After transcribing the first year of our meetings, I was hired as the ghostwriter. I found in these women elements of a fiery enthusiasm, a composed benevolence and a determined can-do confidence. I learned as much about human character as about history. Judi wrote the forward, which inspired me to research the years of the Air Force allocations before Charline's arrival. For the water controversy, we endeavored to narrate those past events in a positive way, from Charline's perspective, and the people who lived through it in Adair Village. For a sense of the uniqueness of Adair, I introduced the land uses of the surrounding area, the history of the fire district, and the current city businesses.

About the illustrations:

Mike McInally's permission to use newspaper photos greatly enhanced the body of illustrations for Adair Diary. Around 2004, I had taken photos for the first city webpage, so I had many pictures of my own to use. I scanned these into my computer, printed them 8x10 grayscale. I traced in black, scanned them again, and merged the two images, then applied a Poster Edges polarization. The font is Times New Roman 13pt. I used Photoshop CS3 for the covers and authored in Microsoft Word on a MacBook Pro laptop.

- Delores Pollard 2016

INDEX

Made in the USA
San Bernardino, CA
18 April 2016